D0673921

THE ARTHUR NEGUS GUIDE TO
ENGLISH FURNITURE

The Arthur Negus Guide to English

FURNITURE

ROBIN BUTLER

Foreword by Arthur Negus

Consultant Editor: Arthur Negus

Hamlyn

London · New York · Sydney · Toronto

For my mother

Published by
The Hamlyn Publishing Group Limited
London · New York · Sydney · Toronto
Astronaut House, Feltham, Middlesex,
England

© Copyright
Robin Butler 1978

First edition 1978
Second impression 1979

ISBN 0 600 33650 6

All rights reserved. No part of this
publication may be reproduced, stored in a
retrieval system, or transmitted, in any form
or by any means, electronic, mechanical,
photocopying, recording or otherwise,
without the permission of The Hamlyn
Publishing Group Limited

Filmset by Keyspools Limited, Golborne,
Lancs
Printed and Bound in Great Britain by
Hazell Watson & Viney Limited
Aylesbury, Bucks

Frontispiece:
Oak buffet or court cupboard, *c.* 1630.

Contents

Foreword by Arthur Negus

Over the past thirty years I have been associated with a firm of fine art auctioneers, Messrs Bruton Knowles and Company of Gloucester, and it has been my pleasure over all those years to prepare their catalogues for auction sales of furniture and fine arts.

It is rather curious to sit facing a company of dealers and collectors at an auction, watching them bidding and trying to assess their individual knowledge. One man, amongst some who stand out in my memory as possessing great knowledge, is Robin Butler. He is an extremely well-known dealer who runs a family antique furniture business in Honiton, Devon. He is exactly the kind of man I wanted to write a book on English Furniture – not just a book showing photographs of museums, but a book imparting his knowledge of woods, of construction and of detail, which form an all-important part in identifying a piece of furniture as being genuinely old. A book which looks inside and underneath, at the flaws and the botched repairs as well as at superb examples of the cabinet-maker's art. As such it will prove of enormous value and help to all those interested in the subject.

This book, together with its companion volume by Bernard Price on English Pottery and Porcelain, forms part of a series of reference books which all use the personal approach to convey the knowledge gained by the authors through years of practical experience in their field.

Arthur Negus

Author's note

Dear Reader,

During August 1977, Arthur Negus asked me if I would write a book on old English Furniture and, after much hesitation and persuasion, I consented. A friend suggested that I would do well to commit to paper those thoughts I had about the subject but that during the gestation and writing of the book, I should refrain from consulting any reference books whatsoever. This is the product of that sound advice.

I make no pretence that this volume contains the fruit of any original or hitherto unpublished research, nor do I boast any stunning revelations on the subject. Rather, this is my expression of what I have learned from others – my colleagues, friends and particularly my family – and what I have taught myself. I have endeavoured to explain the thought process that I use in the daily execution of my work.

To many people I owe a large debt of gratitude and I must particularly mention Elizabeth Norris, Brian Kern and Sheila Miles. Guy Holland proffered numerous most helpful suggestions and John Gaisford created meaningful prose from a plethora of incoherent ramblings. The book owes a great deal to the photographs, most of which are the highly skilled work of Robert Du Pontet.

It is a sad reflection of our society that by revealing the identities of the owners of the illustrated items, I would render them liable to the attention of thieves and for this lamentable reason, they remain anonymous. All of them have shown me enormous hospitality and have met the demands I have placed on them with great kindness. Finally I add thanks in abundance to my long-suffering assistant Suki Osmond.

I do hope you take enjoyment from reading the following pages and if, as a result of your better appreciation of old furniture, you derive greater pleasure from that too, then I shall be a very happy author.

Yours sincerely,
Robin Butler

Introduction

If a group of observers in the year 2000 were to look at a collection of photographs taken by a family in the mid-twentieth century – the snapshot album that many of us treasure – there is a chance that some of those observers would be able to date the album fairly accurately. An engineer would probably date a photo of a motor car to within five years, and a woman interested in fashion could probably make a close estimate by looking at the girls' dresses. Artists would recognise lettering and advertisements – or would they? What about those mirror-posters made today evoking memories of pre-war Ovaltine, Worthington, Rolls-Royce, or Bovril? By the year 2000 these copies will be old themselves and will have accumulated signs of wear comparable to the originals.

The same dilemma confronts furniture experts when they examine an antique. Knowledge of the materials used and the method of construction sometimes permits a confident assessment, but on other occasions the experts will be less fortunate and, despite thorough examination in a good light, will still be left uncertain as to who made the article, where and when. Recently, at a conference of the Furniture History Society, a large group of people were discussing two chests of drawers. Several suggestions were put forward as to the nature of the chests, but the only point on which there was agreement was that *nobody* knew for certain. Yet among these experts were the senior staff from leading British museums as well as dealers, lecturers, authors and collectors.

Fortunately such incidents are rare, and in the following pages I shall lead you through the questions you should be asking yourself when you consider a piece of furniture. The first step is to locate the piece in one of four categories: genuine, reproduction, fake or composite. The *genuine* piece can be defined as an object made at the date that its design would suggest. Thus a chair designed by Thomas Chippendale and made in his workshops in the 1760s is genuine, in exactly the same way as a perspex and stainless steel chair made in the

1960s. However, a chair made by John Smith in 1860 to a 1762 Chippendale design is not genuine, despite its considerable age: it is a *reproduction*.

Reproductions are objects made in the style of an earlier time, even if that style is quite recent. Usually they are sold as such when new, and little or no attempt is made to disguise the fact that the maker is trying to conjure up the feeling of a bygone age. These articles are very often superbly crafted in fine materials. While it is quite acceptable for the polish of a reproduction to be shaded, or even for the surface to be 'distressed', in an attempt to mellow the appearance, this process should not be continued to such a degree that an intelligent, if inexperienced, observer may be excused for thinking that the object is old. Just occasionally, however, the maker tries to simulate the passage of time in his creation, and eventually the point is reached where the intention is to deceive. This type of copy can only be described as a *fake*, and indeed some fakers are so knowledgeable that they can simulate even the finer points known only to the experts. Only considerable experience and advanced science can combat such trickery, and one must be thankful for its rarity.

The fourth and last category of furniture is known as the *composite*. This may be a combination of any, or all, of the above types, individual parts of which have been 'doctored' or 'improved'. During the mid-nineteenth century for example, Renaissance carved oak furniture was highly fashionable. Fragments of original carved panels were often incorporated into lavish Victorian sideboards, and much plain oak furniture of the seventeenth century was newly embellished by the carver's chisel. Hundreds of seventeenth-, and early eighteenth-century oak long-case clocks (unwarrentedly called by the Victorians grandfather clocks) were the subject of such 'improvement' during the nineteenth century.

Also in the composite category can be listed 'part items', such as the top half of a corner cupboard which has been separated from its lower section and hung from the wall as an entity in its own right. Even the stripped pine furniture which is currently very fashionable must be regarded as composite, for nearly all such pieces were originally painted – either to simulate more expensive wood, or in other colours. When the price of furniture was dictated primarily by the cost of materials rather than labour, servants' quarters and humble households were equipped throughout with articles made of pine.

In the course of this book I hope to show you how to place a piece of furniture into one of these four categories. The strongest emphasis will be on observation and on making logical deductions from the available evidence. Antique collectors are like detectives: at any viewing of an auction sale you will notice people pulling out drawers from bureaux and turning chairs upside down, peering at the parts you will never see unless you follow their example. They are looking for the clues which will help them decide what type of item they are looking at – genuine, reproduction, composite or fake. At the same time, I shall be drawing attention to features which allow us to date an item of furniture; and first and foremost among these is the design.

The dating of all domestic art, whether furniture or glass, silver or porcelain, involves committing to memory the *general* shapes of countless different objects. In my definition of the genuine, I mentioned Thomas Chippendale, who designed many chairs of which the majority are similar in general appearance. Plate 1 is an illustration from his book *The Gentleman and Cabinet Maker's Director*. Perhaps you are one of the very few fortunate people who have seen a chair taken exactly from one of these designs; many more readers will have seen chairs similar in feeling and made at almost the same time.

Plate 3 shows two such chairs. The one on the left bears a very strong resemblance to a design in Plate 1, but the chair on the right, although very similar, does not appear in Chippendale's book (nor, for that matter, in the design books of

1 Plate XVI from the 1762 (third) edition of Thomas Chippendale's *Gentleman and Cabinet Maker's Director*, engraved by Miller.

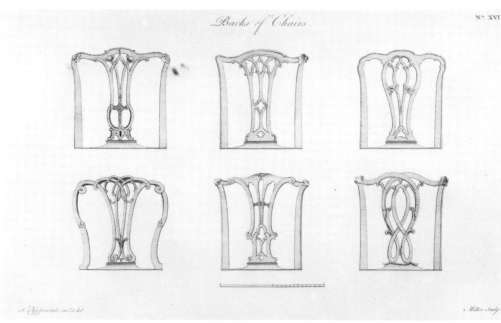

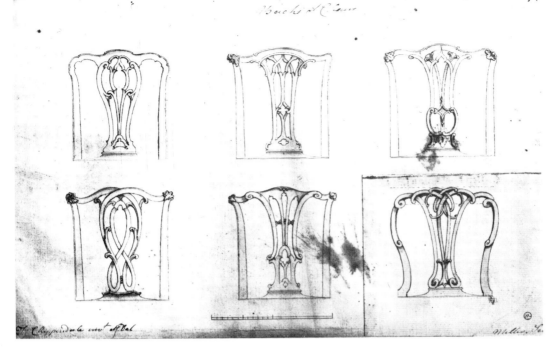

2 The original drawing from which Plate 1 was engraved, now in the Victoria and Albert Museum, London.

any of his contemporaries that I have been able to trace). These are two of perhaps 2000 slightly different chairs, all made at the same time, which are now given the rather nebulous term 'Chippendale'. Thus, while it is important to remember what a 'Chippendale chair' looks like, it is unnecessary to remember each one individually. They all have a resemblance to one another which is quite distinctive; and the same applies to other pieces of furniture.

Quite apart from the designers, external historical factors also affect styles. Furniture historians often mention particular kings and queens, describing items as 'George III' or 'Regency', for the social, financial, religious, artistic and other climates peculiar to each reign seem to have fostered particular aspects of design and craftsmanship. For example, the influx of Huguenot craftsmen during the closing years of the seventeenth century had a profound influence on the evolution of design – not only in furniture but particularly in silver and almost every other form of applied art. It is important to realise, however, that fashions did not change overnight with the death of the ruler, and a piece of furniture described as 'Queen Anne' may well have been made two or three years after the end of her reign. Furniture made after the accession of Queen Victoria, in 1837, is not generally regarded as antique; indeed 1830 is often taken as the latest date for antique. Design

changed fundamentally around this time, and the increasing use of machinery in furniture-making signalled the decline of the craftsman.

The evolution of English furniture is a complex subject, and it is quite possible to write a book just on the development of the chair. Readers who require more detailed information should refer to the bibliography at the end of this book, or visit the splendid collections in museums such as the Victoria and Albert in London and Temple Newsam House in Leeds. My main concern has been to give advice which will be useful in the auction room or the dealer's shop, and this book has been written with practical problems constantly in mind.

The first part of the book deals in broad outline with information that the reader will need to know before looking at individual pieces of furniture. The fundamental turning points in furniture design are put into a historical context, and some of the great names are mentioned at this point. Once the reader has grasped the main development in English cabinet-making however, a knowledge of the materials used and construction techniques will be indispensable, and a brief account of both is included. Advice is also given on how to recognise quality in furniture, what to look for in surface and colour, and how to check condition. Some readers may find this section difficult at

3 Two 'Chippendale' chairs, the left hand one bearing a strong resemblance to the centre top row of Plates 1 and 2. The right hand one though very similar, does not appear in the *Director*.

first, but do not despair! Used as reference, its contents will soon fall into place and greatly enhance an understanding of furniture in general and items you buy, in particular.

The second part of the book takes a close look at specific items of furniture, spaced fairly evenly throughout the period from 1600 to 1830. The object of this section is to show the reader how an expert will approach a piece of furniture at auction or in a dealer's showroom. It gives a 'bird's eye' view of the process by which one arrives at a satisfactory definition, avoiding the pitfalls which await the unwary. A brief chapter on the market place, and how best to get value for money when buying or selling furniture, concludes the volume.

Critics will find many omissions in this book – Charles II cane seat furniture, brass-inlaid Regency rosewood, scrolled paperwork, to name just three. I would have liked to include examples of all these, and much more, but space is at a premium. Consequently I have made a deliberate decision to include only those pieces which illustrate a particular design or method of construction. Readers who require a comprehensive reference book – of which many have already been published are advised to consult the bibliography.

My aim has been to encourage the reader not just to admire a piece of furniture as a good example of a particular period in history, but to *think* about it: good and bad quality, to appreciate line and movement, and to notice, perhaps for the first time, the minutiae of design and detail. To this end I have included many photographs showing specific aspects of construction and decoration; but it must be emphasized that these are no real substitute for 'going into the field' and physically examining as many pieces as possible.

Throughout, I have expressed personal opinions about pieces of furniture of which I have an intimate knowledge. It is my sincere hope that my own enthusiasm for these pieces will become manifest, and I can only hope that readers will derive as much satisfaction from handling similar items. In the second section I have included the occasional reproduction, fake and composite article, in an endeavour to give a cross-section of the type of furniture one may encounter in everyday circumstances. Care has been taken to find examples of the humble as well as the grandiose, and I hope that my enthusiasm for modest charm as well as the virtuoso product will be apparent.

If I can stimulate your interest in English antique furniture, and give a glimpse of how much there is to admire and enthuse over, then this book will have achieved its purpose.

Part one   Chapter 1

Evolution of objects and design

Before the seventeenth century, houses were sparsely furnished, with a very limited variety of articles. The most common items were the coffer, which held everything that today we would put on shelves, or in cupboards and drawers, and the aumbry or hutch. Even chairs were confined to the grander households and reserved for important people; lesser mortals sat on benches or stools. Most tables were of the refectory type and only used at mealtimes, although towards the end of the sixteenth century, a few other tables were being made for games and for placing in smaller rooms such as bed-chambers. The very well-to-do had four-poster beds, which were considered prime status symbols because the drapery was so costly – and this remained true well into the eighteenth century. Rich households may also have boasted portable writing desks and musical instruments.

During the next 100 years, however, these basic forms began to evolve and diverge into the styles we are familiar with today. By about 1620, the dining chair had already emerged: the rear legs of the common stool were simply projected upwards to provide the framework for an upholstered back-rest. The food hutch had been developed into a cupboard designed not only for the reception of food and possessions, but also as a display stand for the family silver and for porcelain, which was beginning to be imported from the Orient. Drawers were incorporated into portable writing desks, and by the end of the seventeenth century the chest of drawers itself became a common object, having first appeared during the 1650s. Travelling desks were kept on top of chests of drawers and tables, for towards the end of the seventeenth century someone decided to marry the two pieces together – resulting in the bureau.

A growing vogue for decoration on furniture coincided with these developments. Some medieval pieces were carved with biblical scenes, or occasionally allegorical subjects; otherwise, the main concession to ornament was iron straps. The most

14

4 A late sixteenth-century oak chair, the back panelled with a carved cresting rail and the arms and seat rails of cacqueteuse shape. The seat slides forward to reveal a commode (the chamber pot being removed through the cupboard door on the other side).

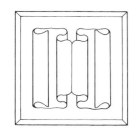

Linenfold

common form of decoration in the late fifteenth and sixteenth centuries was the carving of panels in linenfold. This stylised rendering of drapery was fairly uniform in concept and appears not to have found favour after 1570. Panels carved at this time sometimes had Romayne heads (Plate 5) for alternative decoration.

A technique first used by the Egyptians in the time of Tutunkhamun was re-discovered during the sixteenth century: the art of the inlayer. Chests, or coffers, and the head-boards of four-poster beds are often decorated with holly and bog oak, the white and black of the inlays contrasting sharply with the brown of the oak or walnut into which they are set.

5 *Left*: A Romayne head, or carved portrait medallion, typifying Renaissance influence, sixteenth-century.

6 *Opposite above*: The inlaid back panel of a writing desk c. 1580, typically depicting architectural and geometric designs, probably inspired by Nonesuch Palace. Victoria and Albert Museum.

7 *Opposite below*: Walnut long case clock. The large number of crisp mouldings and intelligent use of halved veneers on the case show its quality. The movement is by George Graham a London clockmaker of the highest calibre.

These decorations often take the form of chevron or chequer lines in a panel, or intersecting triangles and rectangles. Others, on the fronts of coffers and cabinets, depict architecture and, sometimes, the inlay represents Nonesuch Palace, built by Henry VIII and long since destroyed.

During the seventeenth century the use of inlay very soon dropped from favour. Decoration was confined to designs produced by carving or by turning component parts of furniture – such as the legs of chairs and tables – on a lathe. Furniture was first made in this way during the second half of the sixteenth century, and gained importance during the seventeenth century. The flamboyance of the Elizabethan era slowly waned and carving, which was usually confined to gouging, arcading, scrolls and lozenges, became progressively more restrained until the middle of the century.

During the Commonwealth period (1649-60) the Puritan religious influence was so severe that furniture was completely plain, with turning usually the sole concession to decoration. The restoration of the monarchy brought an exuberance unknown since Elizabethan times: carved crowns supported by cherubs abounded. Scrolling and foliage was the

order of the day, and soon even this gave way to marquetry decoration with fruit, flowers and birds in profusion whenever the expense permitted.

The Glorious Revolution of 1688 brought William III from Holland and with him a considerable Dutch influence. William's architect, Daniel Marot, together with the Huguenot craftsmen who came with him, produced designs which were to have a profound effect upon the development of furniture for the next fifty years. The use of new materials, most notably walnut, beechwood and caning for chairs, resulted in new techniques of construction. At the same time, the 'S' scroll became a basic design element for the legs supporting any piece of furniture. Perhaps influenced by designs brought in from the Orient, these were now elongated, and soon developed into the cabriole leg.

The reign of Queen Anne saw a further period of restraint. Carving was abandoned and great importance was attached to symmetry and proportion. Many people consider that the simple furniture of this period is among the finest ever made, with the unadorned cabriole leg the epitome of quiet elegance. The principal timber for fine quality pieces was walnut – cabinet-makers enhanced its attractive natural markings by cross-banding features such as cupboards and drawers and very often offset these with herring-bone or feather banding as well. Walnut particularly lends itself to the production of crisp mouldings both along and across the grain, and maximum advantage was taken of this. However, the harsh winter of 1709 caused havoc with the supplies of walnut and when the governments of producing countries forbade its export in about 1720, the import duties on other foreign timbers were relaxed.

17

8 *Opposite*: Mahogany
cabinet of architectural form
and with crisp carving from
Temple Newsam House,
Leeds. The door and sides are
panelled with needlework.

Mahogany, imported in bulk after 1725, is characterised by
deep tones suitable for furniture of architectural and
monumental proportions. The simplicity of the walnut period
gave way to ornamental features such as pilaster columns and
carved decorated mouldings, such as egg-and-dart, symbolis-
ing life and death (page 166), which were derived from
classical architecture. The straight grain and density of
mahogany also enabled cabriole legs to be made slightly finer
than was possible with walnut, which is softer. Carved
decoration on the knee of a walnut cabriole tends to become
worn with ordinary household usage, but the same decoration
carved in mahogany is more durable. It was not long before
cabinet-makers and carvers recognised and took advantage of
the qualities of mahogany.

The first half of the eighteenth century saw the growth in
Europe of the Baroque, with its emphasis on asymmetry and
ornate, curvilinear shapes suggesting movement. The style

9 Detail of Plate 8 showing
the vigour, crispness and
high quality of the carving
on the cabriole knee of the
cabinet. Temple Newsam
House, Leeds.

20

10 *Opposite*: A Rococo girandole, or looking glass with candlesticks. Note the foliage, scrolls and asymmetric cresting.

never really caught on in England, with a mere handful of admittedly notable exceptions – primarily looking-glasses and console tables *en suite*. Its progeny, the Rococo, however, was an immediate success with asymmetry flourishing amongst foliage, scrolls, icicles and rock-work (from which the name *rococo* is derived). England's most famous exponent of Rococo, Thomas Chippendale, remains a household name. He was a native of Otley in Yorkshire, who served an apprenticeship as a cabinet-maker and moved to London where he set up workshops in St Martin's Lane. In 1754, when he was thirty-six, he produced a book of furniture designs called *The Gentleman and Cabinet Maker's Director* upon which much of his fame still rests. The book served two purposes: first, it informed likely patrons of the styles available for them to choose from; and second, more importantly, it contained working drawings of furniture for cabinet-makers to reproduce his designs – complete with measurements and precise details of mouldings and construction. Chippendale produced furniture to his own designs in the St Martin's Lane workshops where he employed cabinet-makers, upholsterers and

11 Chippendale mahogany wardrobe with carved decoration. The shape of the lower section is said to be 'bombé'.

numerous other tradesmen. He also executed designs to the particular requests of patrons, and many houses such as Harewood, Nostell Priory and Corsham Court retain Chippendale's original bills, which can be correlated with furniture still in the rooms for which it was made. He also supplied carpets, curtains and door furniture (fittings), and today would be called an interior decorator.

During the closing years of the seventeenth century much lacquered furniture had been imported into the country through the East India Company, and interest in the Orient was maintained throughout the eighteenth century. Although Chinese and Japanese lacquering materials were not available in England as they would not travel, work of a lesser quality, commonly called Japanning and popularised by Stalker and Parker, was carried out and a great deal of furniture was made in the Chinese style. Chippendale produced many designs based on Chinese works, which include railings, chairs, cabinets, desks and looking-glasses. Even the thirteen-panel glazed door displays a clear Chinese influence.

By popular demand, and no doubt for sound commercial reasons, Chippendale produced further editions of his book in 1755 and 1762. But Rococo was short-lived in fashionable society and by the time of the last edition, it was already giving way to the Neo-classical. The prime movers of the new style were the brothers Robert and James Adam, who were inspired by their Grand Tour to Italy in the 1750s. Suddenly the outline of furniture became a great deal more simple. The Neo-classic revived the styles of ancient Greece and Rome, where neatness and the symmetrical disposition of set motifs were *de rigueur*. Chief amongst the forms of ornamentation were fluting and oval medallions, anthemion (stylised honeysuckle), sphinx's heads, festoons of garya husks, vases, urns, Greek key patterns, silhouette portraits and the guilloche. The decoration was both carved and inlaid as Neo-classical features still lent themselves to the carver's art, especially the fluting and *paterae* (Plate 13 and glossary).

Being an astute businessman, Thomas Chippendale realised that his earlier advice was now completely out of date, and soon he was co-operating with the Adam brothers in furnishing great houses such as Osterley. George Hepplewhite was another cabinet-maker who followed Adam's lead. His designs appear in *The Cabinet Maker's and Upholsterer's Guide* which was published in 1788, two years after his death, with second and third editions in 1789 and 1794. Among Hepplewhite's many delightful and utilitarian designs one particularly notices the shield-back dining chair (Plate 100), the splayed bracket foot and the revived slender version of the cabriole leg (Plate 41).

Another gentleman who has given his name to an enormous quantity of furniture is Thomas Sheraton. Little is known of his life, except that he was a Baptist minister. He produced the first part of *The Cabinet Maker's and Upholsterer's Drawing Book* in 1791 with designs which were, to a large extent, variations on Hepplewhite's themes, but more advanced. His book contains extremely detailed instructions on perspective drawing and the construction of furniture. Among the many other people producing design books at this time, Thomas Shearer's influence could be said to equal Sheraton's; his *The Cabinet Maker's London Book of Prices* appeared in 1788. Almost all these design books are available in facsimile editions today.

The monumental furniture of the 1730s and 1740s had given way to the decorated style of the Rococo, containing a great deal less wood and thus becoming much lighter. With Neo-classical furniture, the outline had again become simple, and

13 Wine cooler from Osterley Park House, Middlesex. Of carved wood with gilt and metal details, it typifies the Neo-classical movement as designed by Robert Adam. Note the fluting, paterae, medallions, draped rams' heads, the symmetry and, of course, the urn.

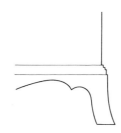

Splayed bracket foot

the proportions were further refined, until a period in the 1790s when tables for example stood on the most slender legs. George Hepplewhite's book even advocated the making of chairs without stretchers to unite and strengthen the legs. Moreover, the quality of cabinet-making in fine, London-made pieces was of such a high order that many survive today in almost perfect condition.

Two influential figures of the early nineteenth century were Thomas Hope and George Smith, who revived the Neo-classical and particularly Egyptian styles. The Regency style 1800-20 (which does not quite coincide with the Regency period 1811-20) was an elaboration of outline, though quite different from Rococo or the earlier Elizabethan and Restoration carved form. Egyptian sphinxes, griffins and hairy paws abounded and with the use of rosewood, satinwood, and gilding a conscious break was made from brown mahogany (Plate 97). The death of Nelson in 1805 plunged the whole country into mourning and resulted in numerous pieces of furniture being outlined with ebony stringing, as a black line of mourning. From this period the inclusion of as much wood and carving as possible became a major feature of fine quality furniture.

14 *Above*: A Victorian credenza (side cabinet) of elaborate and degenerate design. The complicated decoration derives from the work of André Charles Boulle, a maître ébéniste of the late seventeenth-century. This work, however, lacks the quality of earlier examples and much of the detail is mechanical in its concept and execution.

15 *Opposite*: Inlaid mahogany cabinet. While the general outline, especially the shape of the upper section, derives from the Rococo, the decorative detail and in particular the anthemion motifs on the glazing inter-sections and the swags on the cornice show a very clear Neo-classical inspiration. Such pieces are often described as transitional, *c.* 1770.

16 Mahogany displays many variations in appearance, these are the four primary categories. *Top left* the very dense and dark Jamaican wood from a piece of furniture *c.* 1730. *Top right* the brilliantly figured Cuban wood from a chest of drawers *c.* 1770. *Bottom left* a San Domingo mahogany of stripy figure and straight grain from a commode *c.* 1790. *Bottom right* the pale, soft, open-grained Honduras mahogany, the staining and scratches are indicative of its porosity and softness, from a table *c.* 1810.

17 On the left is the straight grained ash, rather more orange than typical. The oak in the middle is an old surface, and with difficulty some medullary rays may be seen evenly distributed over it. The right hand section is elm with the characteristically wavy grain and more broadly spaced annual rings. No photograph can hope to show the variety of any one timber and these are merely fairly typical examples.

18 On the left is a West Indian satinwood – note the similarity between this and Cuban mahogany, although visually the satinwood is much lighter and yellower, and tangibly it is a great deal harder and heavier. On the right is East Indian satinwood which always displays a stripy figure. This example, untypically, dated from about 1800 whereas more commonly this wood appears from *c.* 1880 onwards.

19 *Left*: Brazilian rosewood of characteristic honey colour with black streaks. Note that the grain runs straight through the vivid black marks. From a Regency chiffonière *c.* 1810. *Right*: East Indian rosewood is characterised by darker hues than the Brazilian variety and a relative freedom from contrasting black streaks. Newly cut, is almost black; on prolonged exposure to sunlight it fades to honey. This example is half way, and is taken from a piano, *c.* 1910.

20 An intelligent disposition of four pieces of flame, or crotch, figured Cuban mahogany veneer, taken from four consecutive layers of the same tree. From a Pembroke table top *c.* 1770.

21 Although this writing cabinet does not appear in Sheraton's designs, the bowed ends, turned reeded pilaster columns and spinning-top feet typify his designs, as do the oval panels, quartered veneers, ivory escutcheons and knob handles.

Chapter 2
Timber and other materials

Much furniture today is constructed of leather, stainless steel, plastic and even paper. Tables are made from glass and aluminium, while beds may be filled with water and chairs with haricot beans. In the eighteenth century, however, although beds and chairs were stuffed with horsehair, down, straw and flock, and upholstered in cotton, linen, wool or silk, the rigid parts were usually made of wood. Furthermore, many pieces of furniture like tables or wardrobes were made entirely of timber. It is consequently of great importance to recognise the type of wood employed in any particular piece. Knowledge of the various timbers used in cabinet-making may help particularly in dating an article. For example, if someone claims to have a Queen Anne mahogany chair, they are either mistaken or deliberately trying to deceive. Apart from references to the use of mahogany as ballast in ships returning from the West Indies during Charles II's reign (1660-85), it was not used in England until ten years after Queen Anne died in 1714. The earliest known mahogany furniture dates c. 1725.

In the next few pages, the woods most widely used will be described, approximately in chronological order of the furniture in which they are likely to be found. For the less well-known woods, the reader is directed to a fuller list in the glossary. First, however, a simplified description of the structure of the tree will prove helpful. I shall concentrate on those aspects by which each variety of timber can be distinguished visually from the others. Before going further, one primary distinction must be made. Pine (or 'deal') is the timber from coniferous (or fir) trees and is known as softwood, as opposed to wood from broad-leafed (or deciduous) trees, which is known as hardwood. Softwood is quite different from hardwood and does not show all the characteristics mentioned in this chapter. It is rarely used in good quality furniture, except for back boards and other secondary purposes.

Outside the tropics, where the growing season extends through most of the year, trees grow at an uneven rate. The period of greatest activity is in spring and to a lesser extent the summer; in the autumn and winter trees hardly grow at all. Each year, as they get taller, they put on girth around already established wood. But because climatic conditions change from year to year, the amount of annual growth will vary. Hence when felled and observed in cross-section, trees exhibit rings of uneven width, called annual rings. These are easily seen because the spring growth tends to be coarser in texture than the fine summer wood, and occasionally a dark line separates each year's growth. When a tree is damaged, by fire for example, it heals the wound by producing a lot of extra wood. This occurs at greater than average speed, and so the annual rings are much broader apart, forming an interesting pattern in the timber.

The bark, which forms the outer 'skin' of the tree, is not used in cabinet-making and need be considered no further. Directly underneath is the sapwood, which is paler in colour than the main heartwood and is also softer. Sapwood is seldom used in furniture because it is less strong and is a favourite meal of the woodworm. With certain woods, however, the distinction between sapwood and heartwood is very difficult, if not impossible, to detect with the naked eye.

Running up the tree and out along its branches are fibrous structures like miniature parcels of tubes, each about as thick as a hair. In cross-section, they appear as a cluster of tiny circles; if the cut is made at an angle, they become oval-shaped; and if along the tubes they appear as open grooves. In theory one could cut a piece of wood with grooves running continuously along it, but since trees do not grow absolutely straight, the grooves usually peter out after less than an inch (25 mm).

These tubes are correctly called tracheids and their disposition on the surface of a piece of wood is referred to as the

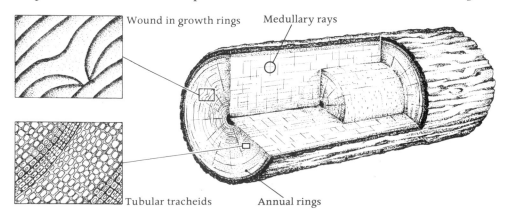

Section through timber

Wound in growth rings   Medullary rays

Tubular tracheids   Annual rings

30

22 The grain on this violin back can just be discerned running along the length of the instrument. The markings which run across the width and join in the middle (the back is made in two pieces) are called figure.

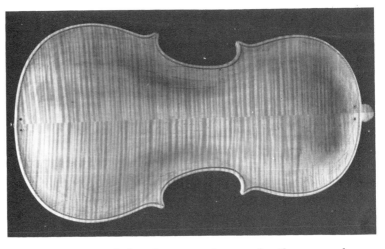

grain. I mentioned that they come in parcels; they grow larger in the spring, and decrease in size as summer progresses. The grain of wood grown in a temperate climate will therefore follow the annual growth rings of the tree, while timber from tropical zones will show a less regular pattern of grain, since the growing season is almost continuous.

A great many types of wood have distinctive patterns or 'figures' which are quite separate from their tracheid arrangement. For example, the grain on the back of a violin runs down its length, in the same direction as the strings. The marking in the wood, however, usually appears to go across the instrument, in a stripy, light-and-dark way that appears to change when the observer and the source of light alter their relative positions. Maple – the wood most commonly used for violin backs – is well known for this particular effect. The same figure appears both in sycamore and mahogany (a totally unrelated tree) and is known – not surprisingly – as fiddle-back figure. Other figures occur frequently and have names, such as feather, flame, curl, roe, plum-pudding and bird's eye, which are all self-descriptive.

While tracheids feed a tree along its length, another system – medullary rays – feeds the girth. Seen in the cross-section of a tree, these are dense fibres radiating from the centre. They are sometimes considerably different in shade from the rest of the wood, and can provide a pattern running at an angle to the grain. In most furniture, however, the medullary rays are difficult to discern.

In the eighteenth century and earlier, a tree to be used for cabinet furniture was first felled and the limbs (or larger branches) removed. A hole was drilled in the butt, or trunk, and a chain inserted in it. This was secured and the trunk

31

allowed to soak in a river for a year. On being taken out it was dried slowly – for two years or so. It was then planked and, depending on the thickness of the plank, it was seasoned at the rate of a year per inch of plank thickness. In this way a man laid the foundation for his son's success. Today the soaking is dispensed with and the drying period is reduced to three to five years, but the seasoning remains the same. All this was important to ensure that the wood warped and split as little as possible.

There are two ways of cutting a 'butt' or tree trunk. The usual method is to cut planks parallel to the diameter. This is quick, and produces the maximum width of planks and therefore return for money. Wood cut in this way is said to be 'run of the mill'– hence our cliché meaning ordinary. Timbers such as oak, where the medullary rays can be seen to advantage, are better 'quarter cut'. This method is expensive but gives the maximum practicable number of cuts that are nearly along a radius. In the Middle Ages the riving iron was used to split wood radially, giving planks of narrow triangular cross-section, and just occasionally one sees a piece of furniture made with wood cut in this way (Plate 59).

From Tudor times specialist sawyers travelled the countryside in pairs, moving from one estate to the next. By manoeuvring the butts across a saw-pit they could cut along the length of even the heaviest trees with a long, two-handled saw – the senior man working above the ground, the junior below. It was hard, monotonous work, demanding considerable concentration, and must have been particularly uncomfortable for the man in the pit. Since the beginning of the century pit-saws have been made redundant by the introduction of large band-saws.

More than once a faked piece of furniture has been discovered for what it is by the tell-tale signs of the machine age. Marks left on timber by imperfections in a band-saw blade, which is always power-driven and fed mechanically, Cutting timber

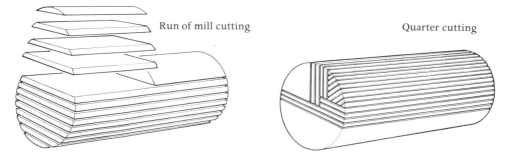

Run of mill cutting · Quarter cutting

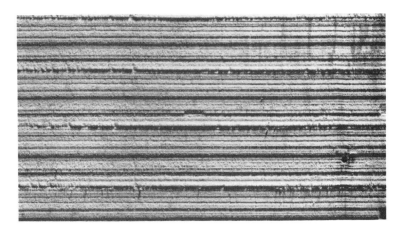

23 Detail of a piece of timber cut with a band-saw. The strong light accentuates the márkings, but they will remain visible wherever a band saw has been used.

will be parallel. Marks left by a pit-saw, by contrast, are somewhat irregular. Perhaps the best place to look for pit-saw marks is on the under-side of seventeenth- and early eighteenth-century oak furniture – under gate-leg table tops of that period and under the tops of dressers and cupboards where there has been no need to finish the wood further.

During the Middle Ages and up to the middle of the seventeenth century, furniture was generally made from wood grown close to the place of manufacture. Most English trees which grow large enough to provide planks can be used for furniture making. They include ash, elm, oak, sycamore, chestnut, beech, birch, maple and walnut. With the exception of oak, all are subject, to a greater or lesser degree, to decay either through rot, or through woodworm or other beetles of that family. Furniture-makers and joiners have long been aware of the lasting properties of oak and used this wood for their better quality wares. Consequently, most of the very early furniture which has survived is made of oak.

24 The underside of a gate leg table top showing the irregularity of the marks left by a pit-saw. The consistency of the majority of the saw marks indicates the expertise of the sawyers. The hinge is held in position with hand-made nails, and is itself hand wrought.

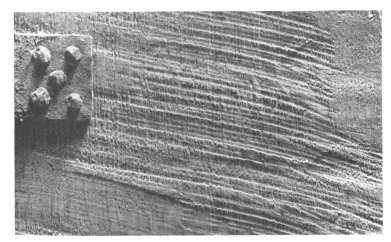

Oak is a heavy wood, ranging in colour from pale straw to that of a brazil-nut shell. The annual rings vary considerably in width and it has very marked medullary rays when quarter-cut – sometimes called 'silver fleck'. On an old surface these usually appear dark, but on freshly cut or re-polished wood they appear many shades lighter than the rest. The medullary rays are also harder and for this reason will occasionally stand proud from surrounding wood. The grain in oak is deep and difficult to fill but otherwise it accepts a polish easily (Plate 17).

Very early furniture is sometimes a mellow, deep straw colour, but late sixteenth- and seventeenth-century pieces tend to be a dark grey-brown, largely due to surface dirt accumulation. Georgian oak tends to be less grey and can even veer towards a reddish-brown, though never as much as mahogany. When used in drawer linings, the lack of light and air keeps oak an ochre hue.

Oak normally exhibits little or no figure. However, when a tree is consistently lopped, growth may accumulate at that point, producing a burr figure known as pollard oak. Another much sought-after variety is so-called brown oak. It has a deeper, red-brown colour, caused by pigment from a large fungus that permeates the whole tree. All oak is hard, and will resist any attempt to depress it with a thumb-nail.

Ash bears a strong resemblance to oak and it can be very difficult to distinguish between the two (Plate 17). The grain of ash tends to be coarser and the wood is marginally softer; it is usually possible to depress the wood with a thumb-nail. Ash is also whiter and the grain is usually straighter. Unlike oak, ash is susceptible to attack from woodworm and the presence of the beetle can often be a sure indication. Very little ash furniture survives from the seventeenth century and later it was employed only in more rustic pieces.

Elm completes the trio of frequently used hardwoods that are problematic to identify. Like ash, elm is susceptible to woodworm and has a very similar density. However, it has a more ginger colour and the grain is broader and usually more wavy (Plate 17). The planks into which it is cut are generally larger than with oak or ash, and farmhouse table tops made of a single plank can be up to 3 feet 6 inches (over a metre) wide.

Walnut has a fine grain: the tracheids are small but often extend for an inch or more along the surface. The medullary rays are very rarely discernible. Perhaps the most distinctive feature of walnut, however, is its basic honey colour (Plate 76), ranging from pale through golden to a deep rich hue, with never a trace of red or grey. Nonetheless, walnut can, and often does, have grey to black streaks and can show some interesting figures. The best known is the burr (Plate 78), taken from growths which are usually formed on the trunk of a mature tree. Walnut can also show mottled figures. It is of medium weight and density, but the evenness of grain makes it an easy wood to work on, whether it is for carving or for cutting into veneers.

Walnut was regarded as a first-grade timber for furniture in the seventeenth century and earlier, but relatively little survives from this period, as the wood is highly vulnerable to woodworm. It was frequently used as a veneer during the first quarter of the eighteenth century, but owing to a severe winter which devastated the walnut tree throughout Europe in 1709 it was little used once the seasoned stocks had been exhausted during the 1720s. Cabinet-makers kept back some of their finest walnut, however, and the few pieces of walnut furniture crafted in the 1730s and 1740s are usually of the finest quality. The timber was eventually re-introduced during the mid-nineteenth century.

Red walnut is similar to the common variety except that it never has burr figures and, true to its name, is red-brown in colour. It is also known as Virginia walnut because it comes from that part of the United States. Red walnut is easily mistaken for mahogany, but since it is grown in a temperate climate, the annual growth rings are quite apparent and the grain provides the pattern. All mahogany is tropical, and the grain passes through any surface pattern. Like mahogany, red walnut is resistant to woodworm and occasionally one will notice sapwood which is golden yellow, usually on insignificant or unseen surfaces, such as the top inside of the back leg of a chair, or the underside of stretchers.

Mahogany is a red-brown timber. It was commonly used in Britain from 1724 and was the wood most used in quality cabinet-making for the next 200 years. If a piece of furniture has a reddish hue, there is a strong chance that it will be mahogany. A strong, fine-grained timber, it shows considerable variation in density and its colour ranges from pale honey to dark plum. Mahogany can be divided for convenience into four main categories (Plate 16).

Jamaican wood, of which the earliest mahogany furniture was made, is very dark and heavy. When freshly cut the wood has an almost purple hue, with characteristic white flecks in the grain. When observed on an unrestored piece, it usually accumulates a greenish, grey-black surface almost resembling bronze where it is not polished regularly. It has little figure and on account of its density and the closeness of its grain is well suited to mouldings and carvings, which remain very crisp. It is said that this early mahogany, seldom seen after about 1745, grew only by the coast and that the supply was used up quickly as it was easier to take wood from the coastal areas than to cut inland through dense tropical forests.

When stocks of the very dense Jamaican wood were exhausted, importers turned to the less desirable *Cuban* wood. This varies little in colour except when subjected to prolonged sunlight and is within a few shades of a reddish tan. Cuban mahogany weighs about half to two-thirds as much as Jamaican wood, but compensates for its lack of density by a considerable range of figure. The most common Cuban figure is the flame or crotch, while more unusual and therefore more sought-after figures are plum pudding, roe, fiddle-back and splash.

San Domingo mahogany is also called Spanish mahogany, as it originally came from the Spanish colonies of the West Indies. It was considered of better quality than Cuban wood and is denser and of a slightly darker hue. It exhibits fewer figures, but is often somewhat 'stripy' or 'cloudy'. The grain tends to be straighter than in Cuban wood and is consequently stronger, making this type of mahogany more suitable for use in fine quality legs and other structural parts. Many experts find the difference between Cuban and San Domingo mahoganies very difficult to perceive.

Honduras mahogany, cut from trees on the South American mainland away from the coast, was also known as baywood. It is quite inferior to other mahoganies, being considerably lighter in colour and density. It has few figures, but during the last quarter of the eighteenth century was considered adequate for drawer linings and other non-visible and utilitarian parts of furniture. Cheaper furniture was made entirely of baywood, which was much used after about 1870 when many of the finer woods were exhausted.

Boxwood and ebony can be considered together, because they are used for similar purposes. Boxwood is a very heavy, dense timber with little figure, and is pale yellow or straw in colour. Ebony is also very heavy and hard, but is almost completely black (though in large pieces yellowish figures appear). Both woods are generally cut into long, thin strips of square cross-section; this is called stringing and provides a perfect edging for furniture. It gives both a contrasting colour, to emphasise the outline, and an edge that will withstand wear. For decorative purposes, ebony and boxwood are used together, often in threes, one sandwiching the other. Sometimes boxwood was replaced by holly, which is not so hard, but almost the same colour, or sycamore which is softer still. Similar economies were practised with ebony, but as no cheaper natural black wood is available, stains and even scorching were employed.

There are two types of satinwood, from the West and East Indies respectively. West Indian satinwood bears strong resemblance to mahogany in its figures, but is much heavier and, except when left unpolished for a long time, is distinctly golden yellow. When freshly cut it emits a sickly, sweet smell and is a pale but bright yellow. West Indian satinwood was generally used as a veneer on quality furniture between 1770 and 1810. East Indian satinwood is also a golden yellow colour and is, if anything, even harder and heavier. Its distinguishing feature is a pronounced 'stripy' figure, which 'moves' easily in different lights. It was introduced to Britain late in the eighteenth century, but is seldom found in furniture of that time. However, it was frequently used in 'Sheraton-style' furniture made between 1890 and 1920 and often provides the first clue in recognising these reproductions.

As with satinwood, there are two varieties of rosewood. The most desirable type comes from Brazil and is also known as Rio rosewood. Its colour ranges from coffee to honey, but the most distinctive features of the timber are black streaks, forming patterns which cut across the grain and finish abruptly. Rio rosewood was introduced almost simultaneously with satin-wood, during the last quarter of the eighteenth century, and is characteristically found in free-standing quality furniture such as sofa tables, teapoys, small tea caddies and work boxes.

East Indian rosewood, from Ceylon and the eastern seaboard of India, was introduced much earlier, being imported by the East India Company and used in cabinets during Charles II's reign (1660-85). Wood of this period, through oxidisation over a very long time, has acquired a similar colour to the Brazilian variety but lacks the black streaks and figure. East Indian rosewood was re-introduced around 1800 and was used extensively during the first sixty or seventy years of the nineteenth century, both as a veneer and in the solid. When an article of East Indian rosewood furniture has been left in strong sunlight for a prolonged period of time it may acquire a pale golden colour, but it started life almost entirely black and an unoxidised wood or re-polished surface will be very dark indeed. Like its Brazilian counterpart it is very heavy and dense, with a broad grain which is difficult to fill and polish.

Chapter 3
The parts of furniture

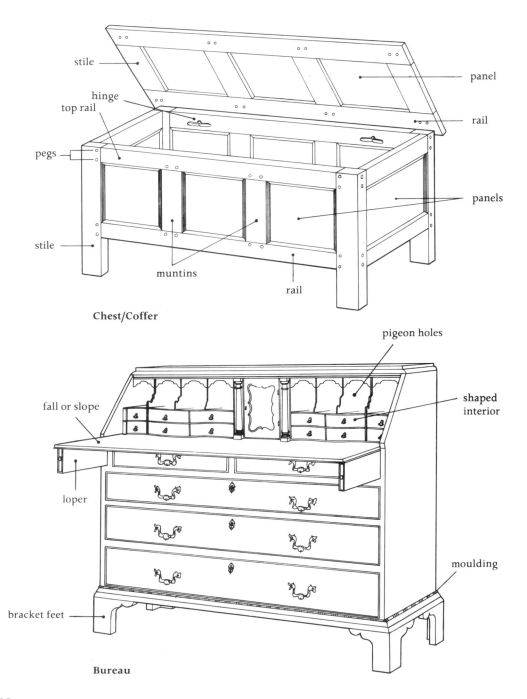

stile

panel

hinge

top rail

rail

pegs

panels

stile

muntins

rail

Chest/Coffer

pigeon holes

fall or slope

shaped
interior

loper

moulding

bracket feet

Bureau

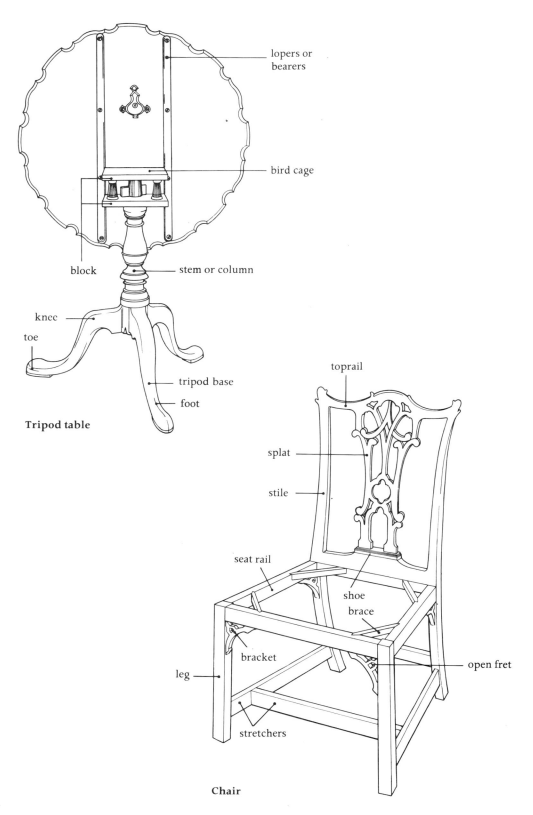

lopers or
bearers

bird cage

block

stem or column

knee

toe

tripod base

foot

Tripod table

toprail

splat

stile

seat rail

shoe

brace

bracket

open fret

leg

stretchers

Chair

Chapter 4
Construction

Over the centuries, the vagaries of fashion and the use of different types of wood brought numerous subtle changes in the methods of furniture construction. The way in which a piece is actually put together will therefore provide valuable clues to the date of its assembly. For example, in the seventeenth century all 'carcase' or 'case' furniture (made to contain cupboards or drawers, as opposed to tables and seat furniture) was made with a panelled construction. This was to cope with the problem of shrinkage, for as timber dries, it shrinks across the width of the grain.

If the average shrinkage is one per cent, then the shrinkage in a board 10 inches (254 mm) wide will be only $\frac{1}{10}$ inch (2.5 mm). This is a negligible amount; but in a piece of wood, or pieces of wood glued together, 10 feet (2.5 m) wide, the shrinkage will be more than an inch (25 mm) – quite impossible to hide in any piece of furniture. By constructing large surfaces from a number of small panels 'floating' in rebates (grooves), the problem can be overcome. In a coffer, for example, the rails, stiles and muntins will all be rebated to hold the panels. When the panels shrink, no gaps appear because the entire width still falls within the rebate.

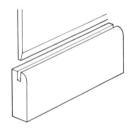

Rebate in a panel

In the seventeenth century glue was not made sufficiently strong to be used in structural joints. Consequently, a system was devised for keeping furniture together without the use of glue, nails (which tend to make wood split and which rust), or screws (which are complicated to make, which also rust, and which were considered suitable only for special purposes). The 'mortise and tenon' joint became the principal method of constructing furniture. The mortise is a rectangular hole cut into one piece of wood (it may not go right through) and the tenon is a tongue cut in the adjoining piece of wood to slot directly into the mortise. In certain parts of England the tenon is called the 'tenant', which is a good way of remembering that the tenon (tenant) lives in the mortise.

Well made, such a joint will hold by itself, but it can easily

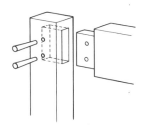

Mortise, tenon and peg

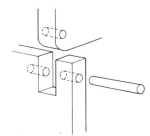

Pin hinge

Wire hinge

Six-board coffer with strap
hinge

be knocked apart. In the sixteenth century, to avoid this happening, a hole was drilled right through the mortise and tenon and a piece of green (unseasoned) timber driven in. This green wood was called a peg and was usually about $\frac{1}{4}$ inch (6 mm) in diameter. The timber of houses of that date was held together in the same fashion, the pegs in this case being anything up to an inch (25 mm) across. During the seventeenth century it became the norm to double up on this procedure and two pegs will be found in each member in most furniture, unless the piece of wood holding the tenon is very small.

In panelled furniture of the period, pegs will be found at the junction of each stile and rail. It should be noted that a stile always continues to the top of the joint, and that the rail always tenons into it. A piece of furniture where the rail runs the entire width and the stile tenons into the rail should be regarded with considerable suspicion, but such construction is not entirely unknown. The muntins will, of course, tenon into the rails and will usually be held by pegs, although during the eighteenth century this practice was sometimes dropped. In a coffer the same construction will apply to the top and side panels, and probably the back also. The lid will closely resemble the construction of the front, but will not be carved.

In very early coffers the lid was pin-hinged, but during the late sixteenth century it became fashionable to use wire hinges, which were simply two interlocking loops of wire. Contemporary with both was a third form of hinge, used when more security was desired: the long strap-hinge. This is more like the modern form of hinge, with the stationary section short and broad, and the other part a long, tapered piece of iron, very often with a decorative end. Eventually it was realised that the strap-hinge was the most satisfactory, as its dimensions could be adjusted to suit the needs of both security and decoration. Old strap-hinges were hand wrought, and this will be evident on close inspection.

One variety of coffer required the least knowledge of construction techniques of any piece of furniture: the very simple, long rectangular box known as a six-board coffer. The front and back were fixed to the ends with nails, and the ends projected downwards to form the feet. Wire hinging was common, although strap-hinges are quite often encountered. Until recently coffers were of relatively little value unless they dated from the sixteenth century or earlier. Later items are very numerous, and are a good subject for study as they were not considered worth altering or 'improving'. Although there are now a great many reproductions and fakes in existence, a large proportion are genuine pieces of seventeenth-century oak furniture and a detailed study of the colour, surface, construction and type of timber is to be recommended.

The chest of drawers was constructed in much the same way as a panelled coffer. The stiles were mortised and the rails, which divided the drawers, were tenoned into them. The sides were also panelled and the top was pegged to the rails. Mouldings might be applied at various points on the carcase to give a decorative finish. Tables and chairs were held together in a similar way with pegged mortises and tenons, and the same was true of beds, cradles, stools and cupboards (Plates 4, 52–61), which constitute almost the entire repertoire of the joiner's art – such furniture was often described as 'joyned' or 'joynt'. By 1715 in London, however, or 1740-50 in remote country areas, better glues had been developed and the peg was usually omitted from mortise and tenon joints. It was retained only where considerable stress could be anticipated – for example, at the top of chair legs.

During the last fifteen years of the seventeenth century two other important techniques had been developed. The first was the use of veneers. This merely involves gluing a thin piece of wood (the veneer) on to a thicker piece (the ground). A large area could thus be covered cheaply with fine quality wood, and if two or more pieces of consecutive veneer were taken from the same cut, they could be arranged to form a decorative pattern with their figure. Veneers varied from $\frac{1}{8}$ inch (3 mm) down to as little as $\frac{1}{16}$ inch (1.6 mm) thick, becoming finer as techniques improved. By the early eighteenth century the use of veneers was already widespread. The general rule is that the thicker the veneer the earlier it is. In the eighteenth century veneers were hand sawn and, as techniques improved, the thickness diminished from $\frac{1}{8}$ inch to $\frac{1}{16}$ inch (3 mm to 1.6 mm). By the nineteenth century the machine age enabled the production of mechanically sawn veneers less than $\frac{1}{16}$ inch (1.6 mm), and by the twentieth century veneers were mechanically knife cut to paper thinness.

The second technique was a new way of joining two pieces of wood at right angles, and was known as the dovetail. This joint uses a minimum of glue and was very satisfactory for joining the sides to the top and bottom of a piece of furniture. It was now possible to abandon the long established mortise and tenon, for which the wood always had to be more than an inch (25 mm) thick and often as much as two inches (50 mm). With this new technique the proportions of carcase furniture were radically altered, for it was now possible to have the sides of a

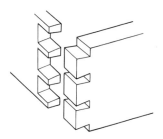

Dovetail

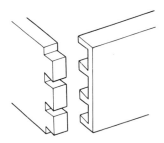

Lapped dovetail

chest of drawers no more than $\frac{3}{4}$ inch (19 mm) thick and strips of wood dividing the drawers could be rebated into them. The drawers could extend to within a fraction of an inch of the side of the object concerned.

The greatest application of the dovetail, however, was in the construction of the drawers themselves, and developments here make the observation of drawers of particular value in dating carcase furniture. Indeed, it is quite possible to date a piece by the construction and material of the drawer alone to within twenty years and sometimes even closer.

Until about 1680 the drawer front was rebated at each end and the sides (linings) were fixed into the rebates with nails. The bottom of the drawer was nailed and rebated into the front and also nailed to the bottom of the linings. The sides had to be at least $\frac{1}{2}$ inch (12.7 mm) and sometimes as much as $\frac{7}{8}$ inch (22 mm) thick, for a groove almost $\frac{1}{2}$ inch (12.7 mm) square was cut right along the drawer, half way up each side. These grooves slid along square wooden runners fixed inside the carcase between the front and back stiles, thus supporting the weight of the drawer. (Curiously enough, this method has enjoyed a revival since the Second World War.) It was customary for the bottom of the drawer to have the grain running from back to front unless the drawer was very wide, in which case it ran from side to side. Drawers in good quality pieces have linings made of oak; pine is more common for rustic pieces, in which case considerable wear will almost certainly be in evidence and one should look for a replacement runner on the upper surface, which takes the weight of the drawer. Oak-lined drawers are known to run quite smoothly even after three or four centuries and, unless the drawer is very deep or has contained heavy things, one would not expect very much wear.

By the 1680s, the dovetail was in common use for better quality drawers. At first the dovetails ran straight through to the front of the drawer and, in order to hide them, a moulding was placed around the front edge. This probably gave rise to the geometrically-panelled chest of drawers with which oak collectors are so familiar – a simple expedient so the cabinet-maker could hide his dovetail joint. At the same time the side drawer-runner became obsolete, for a flat piece of wood fixed to the carcase, reaching from the front to the back, beneath each drawer, proved sufficient to take the weight. The drawer bottoms now had to be fixed to the lining by rebates and glue, for nail heads running on the drawer divide would soon cause damage. With this new construction it was possible to make the drawer linings narrower, first to a bare $\frac{1}{2}$ inch

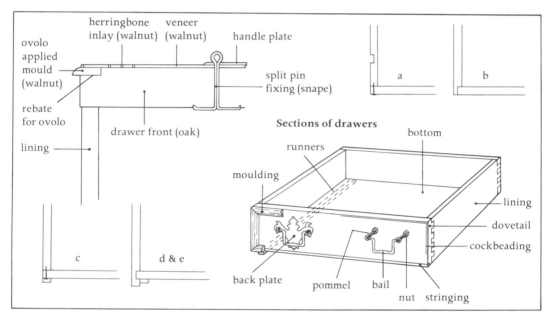

ovolo
applied
mould
(walnut)

rebate
for ovolo

lining

herringbone
inlay (walnut)

veneer
(walnut)

handle plate

split pin
fixing (snape)

drawer front (oak)

c

d & e

a

b

Sections of drawers

moulding

runners

bottom

lining

dovetail

cockbeading

back plate

pommel

bail

nut

stringing

25 (a) Drawer, *c.* 1620. Because the drawer is very wide the grain runs from side to side. Note the front rebate and the sides nailed into the rebate, and the side runner. (b) Veneered drawer front *c.* 1690. Points to note are the dovetails running right through the drawer front and only covered by the thickness of the veneer. The grain of the drawer bottom runs from back to front. The linings are of quarter-cut oak (with the medullary rays visible) and their tops are flush with the top of the front. The handle is not original. Notice the broad, but well made, dovetails. (Ann Eame was the original owner of this piece, and her name appears in several places.) (c) Drawer from a country-made piece of furniture. The drawer bottoms 'incorrectly' go from side to side. The broad dovetails are crudely put together, do not extend to the front of the drawer and are not hidden by the moulding. The linings

have round tops, and the drawer front stands proud of them. *c.* 1720. (d) Well-made country drawer, *c.* 1725. Note the pine drawer linings, broad dovetails and, in contrast, the quality of the original brass handle and mitred cross banding on the drawer front. Note also the ovolo mould to the edge of the drawer and the step down from the drawer front to the linings. (e) Fine quality small drawer, *c.* 1720. The similarity between this and the previous one is obvious, but note the finer dovetails and the use of oak as a drawer lining. The ovolo mould overhangs the linings and the top edge to form a dust excluder. The quality is also shown in the engraved plate handle, figured drawer front and use of feather banding in addition to cross banding. Note also the fixing of the lock. (f) Drawer *c.* 1770. The grain on the bottom runs from side to side. Note the finer dovetails, and particularly the use of

44

c

d

e

f

the cockbead to edge the drawer front. The linings are thin and of quartered oak, notice the scribing line at the end of the dovetails. (g) London-made drawer, *c*. 1800. Note the exceedingly fine dovetails and the drawer front outlined with stringing. The stringing on the top of the drawer front extends to the back of the drawer front, a feature indicating great quality. The grain of the drawer bottom runs from side to side. The wooden handle knob is original and the drawer sides are of Honduras mahogany.

g

(12.7 mm) and over the next 100 years to as narrow as $\frac{1}{8}$ inch (3 mm). This gradual narrowing was progressive, and is a distinct aid in the dating of drawers. During the last years of the seventeenth century it became possible to relinquish the moulding which covered the dovetail, and instead the whole drawer front was veneered.

By 1690-1700 the dovetails no longer extended right through to the veneer and their shape was also changing. Viewed from the side of the drawer, the dovetails had been broad at first, but they gradually became narrower. By the mid-eighteenth century dovetails were ending in a point, and the frequency with which the joints appear along a given length of a drawer side became an indicator of quality. The scribing line, made by the cabinet-maker when preparing to cut his first dovetail, frequently remains for us to see today. It was of course always scribed, never drawn with a pencil.

During the first half of the eighteenth century, when drawer linings were $\frac{1}{4}$–$\frac{3}{8}$ inch (6–9.5 mm) wide, it was customary for the drawer lining to be $\frac{1}{8}$ inch (3 mm) shallower than the drawer front, forming a distinct step down from the top of the drawer front to the top of the drawer lining, and to have the grain of the drawer bottom running from side to side. This was not a firm rule, however, and in several genuine pieces different drawer linings even run from back to front and from side to side within the same piece of furniture.

By about 1720-25, it became the practice to fit the drawer bottom into a rebate $\frac{1}{8}$ inch (3 mm) from the base of the linings and front. The projecting linings then had a strengthening fillet some $\frac{1}{2}$–$\frac{3}{4}$ inch (12-20 mm) wide along their perimeter and the drawer slid along these runners. Usually the fillet was 'mitred' – cut at an angle of 45° – at the back. Drawers of this construction run far more smoothly than the earlier types because the area in contact with the carcase is reduced. Lubricated well with candlewax they will last a great many years with almost no wear at all. However, owners have not always treated their furniture well and the amount of wear on drawer runners may testify to the age of the drawer, or at least indicate whether or not it is a reproduction.

The method of finishing the edge of a drawer front is a further guide to the age of a piece. Mention has been made of the geometrical mouldings applied to the front of furniture during the third quarter of the seventeenth century. When veneers were first used they were usually banded to make a decorative border and the veneer simply ran to the edge of the drawer. A moulding, half round as a rule, was applied to the

46

carcase and thus drew attention to the shape of the drawers. Later this half round was doubled up, yet still the drawer front remained perfectly flat (Plates 61 and 69).

By about 1700-20 it was common to rebate the edge of the drawer front and to apply an ovolo moulding; the joint between the rebate and the moulding was covered with veneer. For a very short while the ovolo mould finished flush with the top and sides of the drawer, but soon it overlapped the carcase so that when the drawer was pressed home it formed an effective dust excluder. By about 1720 the most common of all drawer finishes had been evolved – the cockbead. The drawer front was simply rebated to the depth of $\frac{3}{8}$ inch (9.5 mm) all the way round its perimeter and the rebate, approximately $\frac{1}{8}$ inch (3 mm) wide, was filled with a piece of wood which protruded some $\frac{1}{16}$ inch (1.6 mm) from the drawer and was rounded on the front edge.

During the second half of the eighteenth century drawer linings in quality furniture became progressively finer. Occasionally the decoration on the front of the drawer, if veneered, would form the drawer edge, but the cock bead remained in vogue until after the turn of the century. From about 1770 some good quality furniture had drawer linings made of cedarwood, and from as early as 1740 mahogany was occasionally used for small drawers in the finest pieces and in box toilet mirrors. In the best walnut furniture drawer linings were themselves made of walnut. Channel Island furniture often has linings made of chestnut wood, while Irish pieces frequently have drawers lined in elm and birch. Many Irish chests of drawers have three drawers across the top instead of one or two as in English examples.

By about 1780 it became fashionable to inlay furniture with boxwood and ebony stringing, thus strengthening the edges with very tough and durable timber. In most cases the cock bead gave way to a boxwood stringing; but in the finest London-made examples, the boxwood sometimes covers the entire top of the drawer front. Such pieces may also have $\frac{1}{4}$ inch (6 mm) quarter-round beading along the inside bottom edge (also known as a quadrant dust bead), and if the drawer is wide enough there will be a central muntin as well. This form of construction had itself become common by about 1800.

The earliest form of handle for drawers and cupboards was the wooden knob, although many cupboards were opened and closed with a key only. By the seventeenth century the use of iron handles had become widespread. Their form varied very little for at least fifty years. By the end of the century, however, brass was beginning to be used. The first designs followed continental fashion, often an elongated pear-shaped (or bifurcated scroll) drop with a back plate behind. During the 1690s a six-pointed star was popular.

By 1700 it became fashionable to have a bail handle, simply a 'C' scroll-shaped piece of brass with a lug at either end so it could rotate upon its long axis. Both the bail handle and the earlier pear drop were fixed to the drawer front by a snape which was bent back on the inside of the drawer front and secured. With the bail handle came the introduction of the back plate, which protected the drawer front from being scratched by the hand as the bail was grasped. Early back plates were of shaped outline but not pierced; they were cast with bevelled edges and often decorated with punched circles.

By about 1715, back plates were mostly plain; they tended to be more curvilinear, but still with bevelled edges. The next development, in about 1720, was the piercing of the back plate and at this stage it became larger and more fanciful, though still

26 Drawer handles
1. Iron drop handle with heart pull and quatrefoil backplate. Iron snape fixing, *c.* 1650.
2. Brass 'Dutch drop', engraved quatrefoil backplate – note the snapes, *c.* 1680.
3. Bifurcated drop, gilded hexafoil backplate – thick snapes not original, *c.* 1690.
4. Escutcheon – gilt punched brass – note solid appearance and bevelled edge.
5 and 5a. Backplate and bail, dull brass bevelled edges – note fluency of curves, *c.* 1720.
6, 6a, 6b. Backplate, bail and matching escutcheon – very elaborate non-pierced type – note differences between backplate and escutcheon – fixing holes, etc, *c.* 1730.
7 and 8. Two escutcheon cum backplates (for short drawers with central handle and lock) – early pierced handles bevelled on all edges – usually gilded.
9 and 10. Two more for a similar use to 7 and 8, but note the greater elaboration with 'Chinese Fret' influence.
11, a, b, c, and d. Gilded cast Rococo handle with cast bail. Note the turned pommel and circular nut fixing. The taller escutcheon en suite comes from a bookcase cupboard door, it is not a drawer escutcheon which would match the handle backplate, *c.* 1755.
12, a, b, c and d. A simple cast and gilt Rococo handle, but the backplate now has two separate rosettes. Escutcheon suitable for cupboards and drawers, *c.* 1765.
13. The simplicity of the classic swan-neck, *c.* 1790–1800. (See also Plates 69, 90.)
14. Brass oval plate handle with matching escutcheon.

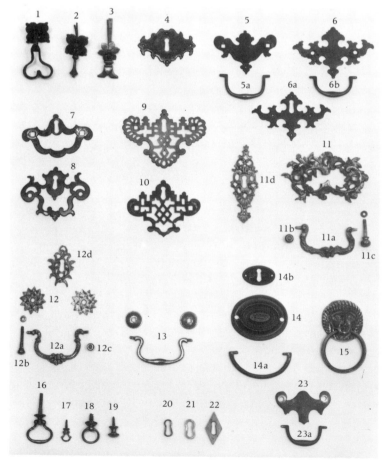

Note the new shape of the bail with inward facing lugs. Gilded, c. 1800.

15. Sphinx head mask and ring handle. Gilded pressed brass. Alternative versions are lion masks and satyr masks. The pommels are integral with the backplate, c. 1800.

16. Intertwined 'C' scroll handle, probably from a night commode cupboard, c. 1770.

17. Diminutive gilt brass with wood screw, similar to 16. From the small interior drawer of a bureau, c. 1790.

18. Gilt brass pommel and ring from a bureau loper or brushing slide of a chest of drawers. Note hand-made thread to the screw with its abrupt end, c. 1750.

19. Brass knob, c. 1810. Very similar shapes were used about 1720, but notice the tapered, machine-made screw indicating a late date.

20 and 21. Skeleton escutcheons, c. 1760–90.

22. Bone lozenge escutcheon, probably Irish, often found on flamboyant furniture of second-rate quality, c. 1800.

23. Modern reproduction of a type of handle of circa 1730. Note the unfluent curves and gawky outline, the lack of gilding and no bevels on the edge. The oxidisation of the brass looks very 'forced'. Compare marginal differences of the bails with 5 and 6.

plain and bevelled on both the pierced and outside edges. The unadorned handles were cast and were usually approximately $\frac{1}{16}$ inch (1.6 mm) thick, reflecting the simple designs of furniture in that period. By 1740, with the introduction of the Rococo, handles and backplates became more ornate. Chippendale's design book, amongst others, illustrates enormous handles made of cast brass, although flat handles continued to be made to a slightly more complicated design, reflecting Gothick or chinoiserie style.

In about 1770 handles again became simple and perhaps the classic of handle design, the swan-neck, was introduced. The back plate was reduced to plain roundels and the bail, instead of being a simple 'C', developed into a pair of conjoined ogee curves – hence the expression 'swan-neck'. These remained in fashion for a long while, but the Neo-classical style of Adam brought with it a re-introduction of the back plate handle, now in a different form with Neo-classical ornament; the oval was much in demand. Instead of being cast, these handles were usually pressed from fine brass sheets and it was now quite possible to achieve very crisp designs. Oval back plates often depict trophies of acorns, agricultural instruments and even nationalist themes such as the victories of Nelson or the Scottish thistle. Pressed back plates could also be rectangular or shaped rectangular in outline.

Cast handles were still made, and it is interesting that on furniture such as sideboards, whose light cupboard doors may have handles made from pressed brass, the heavy cellaret drawers would be cast in the same design, giving them the additional strength needed. The Neo-classical period also produced the ring handle, replacing the bail with a single loop pivoting about its uppermost point. The wooden knob was reintroduced in about 1790. At first it was used only on small drawers such as those found on music canterburies, drum tables or whatnots. By the 1820s, however, the knob had become very popular and remained in vogue for the rest of the century. The handles on bureau lopers and very small interior drawer fitments were small brass knobs. By the middle of the eighteenth century, they were conjoined 'C' scrolls, but by the century's end again become diminutive brass or ivory knobs.

Seventeenth-century handles were usually held in place, not with nuts and bolts, but with a split pin either of brass or steel and always narrow in cross-section (Plates 25c and e). This 'snape' method had been abandoned by about 1710. It was replaced by the pommel, a piece of metal with a screw at one end and a ball at the other. A hole was drilled through the ball

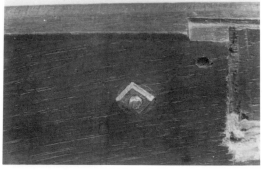

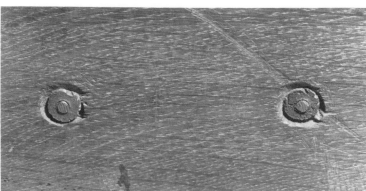

27 Methods of fixing drawer handles. (a) Snape fixing seen from inside the drawer in Plate 25 (c). Snapes are usually longer and are often punched into the wood. (b) Square nut fixing common *c.* 1730-1770. Note the bevelled edge to the hand cut nut and the hand cut thread and pommel. This plate shows the inside of the drawer illustrated in Plate 25(b) and the mark on the right of the handle is a rebate to accommodate the lock, now missing. (c) Circular recessed handle fixing nuts. This variety usually had a slot where a special screw driver was used to secure the nut. The saw mark is probably the work of a ham-fisted restorer and indicates that the handle could have been taken off and replaced at some time.

to accommodate the bail. Apart from early eighteenth-century pommels, where the head is unadorned, these were usually stamped with a circular, turned decoration. They were held in place by a square brass nut with a bevelled edge. By about 1770 the square nut gave way to the circular nut, often with a screw-driver incision. This required the use of a special screw-driver with a notch, to straddle the pommel coming through the nut.

If drawers are used a lot the handles wear out and, as it can be very difficult to find a matching replacement, this can mean replacing the entire set. It is not surprising therefore that relatively few pieces of eighteenth-century English furniture survive with their original handles. During the nineteenth century a considerable amount of furniture was refitted with wooden knob handles and it is only quite recently that the original type of handles have been considered aesthetically worth restoring. When a dealer removes the knobs to replace them with handles appropriate to the design, this usually reveals marks made by the knobs – if not by their fixing, then by their outline. It may even be necessary to make a third set of handle holes, although it is preferable to use the original holes if possible.

Sometimes the restorer is fortunate in that one of the original holes was used for the fixing of a wooden knob, in which case

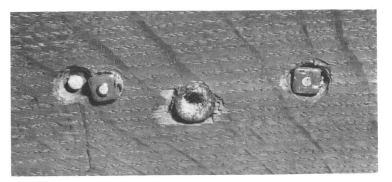

28 Here is evidence of at least three sets of handles having been used. The extreme left hand hole and the right hand hole appear to be original, the left hand one now being filled with a block. The central mark was made by a Victorian wooden knob. This was replaced with another handle using one of the original holes. The wooden knob was sawn off on the front surface of the drawer, but because the replacement handle was not as wide as the original, another hole had to be drilled on the left. Compare these machine-made nuts with the hand-made ones in Plate 27. This whole surface is a clear example of tawdry restoration. (The diagonal marks in the timber are the medullary rays of the oak.)

there may be very little evidence that the piece has had more than one set of handles. Since handles are usually removable, it is often a good idea to take one off if there is any doubt as to whether they are original, and see if there is any sign of holes or marks left by previous sets. On one such occasion I noticed that there were three sets of handle holes at the back of the drawer front, but only one set on the front. This was clear evidence that the piece of furniture had had the drawer fronts re-veneered using old wood.

Locks will be a small help in dating. Seventeenth-century locks tended to be steel, and upwards of 3 inches (76 mm) across and almost square, held in place with nails. They became progressively smaller and by about 1720 were usually a bare 2 inches (51 mm) square on fine domestic furniture, although larger on pieces of massive proportions. By 1740 brass was used as well as steel, being considered more decorative, and locks were held in position with screws, the drawer front being rebated to accept the lock.

The piece of brass that surrounds the key-hole is called an escutcheon, unless it follows the shape of the key-hole and is very narrow indeed, in which case it is simply called a skeleton key-hole or skeleton escutcheon. When a key is inserted in a lock it is very rare for a key to locate on its pin at once without striking the drawer front, and the escutcheon protected the

29 From left to right: Steel lock, *c.* 1720. Brass lock, *c.* 1780 (note the steel wards on the back plate). Steel lock *c.* 1780 (note the long shoot). Bramah lock *c.* 1800 (note the absence of ward marks on the back plate and the name on the top). Victorian lock, *c.* 1880 (note the writing on the top plate – 'Secure patent three lever' – and absence of wards).

drawer from this damage. By about 1770 escutcheons for the first time varied in size from the back plates and became diminutive interpretations of the larger designs.

During the nineteenth century locks were patented, and impressed letters saying 'patent' or 'secure', or even royal cyphers, indicate a late date of manufacture. The drawer itself may be earlier, if it has been refitted at a later date with another lock, but this is a point which should be checked when encountered. Bramah locks were fashionable for good quality furniture, but this company was not founded until 1784 and it is very rare to find one of their locks before about 1800. They became very popular, especially for desks, in the mid-nineteenth century.

The bookcase is one item of carcase furniture which may not have drawers, and we must look elsewhere for indications of quality and date. Most bookcases have adjustable shelves to accommodate different size books. In early examples, strips of wood often no more than $\frac{1}{4}$ inch (6 mm) thick are applied to the sides of the bookcase at regular intervals, and the shelves rest between these fillets. With the introduction of close-grained mahogany it was more common to rebate the sides and the shelves slide into the grooves. The top and bottom of the bookcase itself were normally fixed to the sides with a series of dovetail joints, which give great strength in a lateral direction and form a brace against the outward thrust of the shelves. Both fillets and rebates normally stop short of the top and bottom of the bookcase by about 4-9 inches (102-229 mm). If they run right to the top, this may indicate that the piece has been reduced in height to fit a room with a lower ceiling.

In the early part of the nineteenth century there was a new development. Each side was drilled with two rows of corresponding holes, one at the front and one at the back. Small wooden pegs shaped like button mushrooms were inserted into these holes and these supported the shelves. In some cases metal pegs were used, which were closer in shape to a violin peg, but smaller; the shelves were drilled at each end with a recess which locked on to the peg. This method of support was invisible at a casual glance.

The thirteen-panelled glazed door is a very common way of finishing bureau bookcases and cabinets. The glazing bars should be approximately $\frac{1}{8}$ inch (3 mm) wide and rebate a similar depth into the stiles and rails. Sometimes the rebate is hidden, if the glazing bars are tenoned into the stiles and rails, but this rarely occurred before about 1800. Early glass makers could not produce large sheets of glass, which was made by

30 *Above*: Glazing bars, *c.* 1780. The wide piece on the left hand side is the stile of the cupboard door of the corner cupboard in Plate 93. The thin piece of wood entering it is a glazing bar and can be seen to rebate into the stile. The bevel between the glazing bar, stile and the glass is the putty holding the glass. Old putty becomes rock hard. *Opposite*: Glazing bars, *c.* 1800. A similar section from the bureau bookcase in Plate 95. The stiles stand proud of the glazing bars which mortise into it.

blowing a bubble or cylinder, then cutting this open and laying it flat on a 'table'. The size of a pane was thus determined by the power of the maker's lungs. Such glass is very thin, perhaps $\frac{1}{16}$ inch (1.6 mm), and is never completely flat. It is secured into bookcase doors with putty, which is stained to a dark brown. New putty takes months to harden and restoration, even using old glass from a picture for example, may therefore be noticeable for some considerable time. Expert craftsmen using special materials, however, can readily simulate the appearance of age.

The first mirrors of glass appeared with the restoration of the monarchy in 1660. The plates seldom exceeded 15 inches (380 mm) in any one direction, and were generally surrounded with intricately shaped frames of stump work, bead work, straw work, silver and so on. Looking glasses of the early eighteenth century were also most valuable objects and were still novelties in their time. Any mirror longer than 3 feet (1 m) in any direction had to be made of more than one plate, and until the middle of the eighteenth century it was impossible to make large mirrors with silvered plates. The edge of a plate was usually bevelled, but on old bevels, the angle is very shallow and should hardly be detectable when you run your finger across the apex. The glass will also often be quite striated on the bevel.

Even today bevelling is a long and expensive process, but it is a most satisfactory way of finishing a plate. For about ten years either side of 1700 plates were often decorated with cutting or stars. Early mirrors are thin, and this can be tested by touching the surface with a finger or a sharp object. Observe how far the reflection is from the object. With old glass it should appear little more than $\frac{1}{8}$ inch (3 mm) away, but with modern glass which is often twice as thick the image will appear $\frac{1}{4}$ inch (6 mm) away. The distance of the image will always be double the thickness of the glass.

Moving on from carcase furniture, we find that tables are most readily distinguished by the construction of the legs. These are fixed at their upper ends by an arrangement of rails running between them, and the rails are held together by mortise and tenon joints. If the table dates from the seventeenth century or earlier, the framework will be held together with an arrangement of pegs, and the top will be fixed to the framework in a similar fashion. The only rails not united by a pegged mortise and tenon will be those which are accommodating the drawers.

Glue replaced the use of pegs in the early eighteenth century

Shelf arrangements

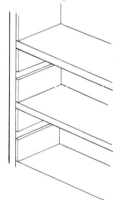

18th-century type

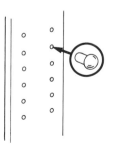

19th-century fixing

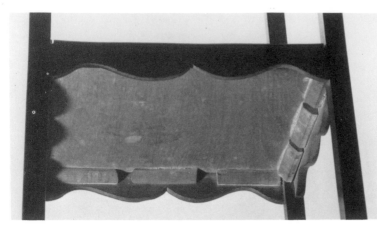

31 Glued blocks on the undersurface of the tray of a whatnot. Note the canted edges and that the surface glue has perished around the perimeter of the blocks.

and from that date it was customary to hold the top with glued blocks: small strips of square timber canted on one edge, with one surface stuck to the top and another to the rail. By the 1740s an alternative method was also being used: the side rail was gouged out to within $\frac{1}{2}$ inch (12.7 mm) of the top and a screw sunk through this recess into the top. Unfortunately (at least for dating purposes) this method of making tables, or a combination of the two, has been used ever since, and it is only in the second half of the twentieth century that resin-based glues have been made in sufficient strength to replace the old form of construction.

Pie-crust table tops and trays are cut and carved from a solid piece of wood, in contrast to modern reproductions where the pie-crust is generally applied afterwards. Trays and little tables which have thin wavy edges or fretted galleries are made with plywood. The wood (mahogany, as a rule) is cut into veneers, two sections going along the grain, sandwiching a cross-grain centre section. The gallery is then rebated into the tray or table top and cut to its wavy shape. The top edge, where the ply

32 The undersurface of a table top, showing the gouge and its screw holding the rail to the top.

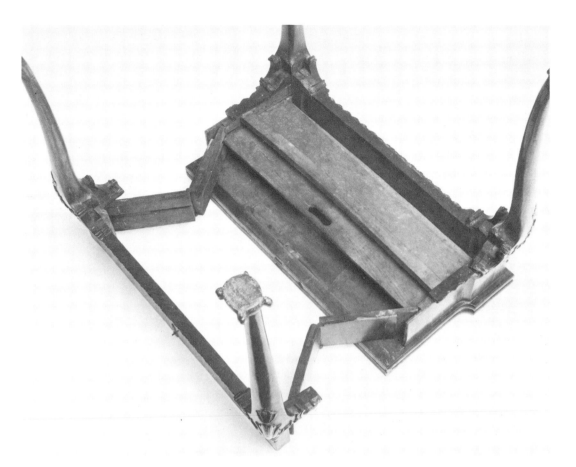

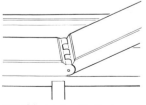

Knuckle joint with fly leg

33 The undersurface of a concertina action card table, half opened. When fully extended, the uppermost of the two braces (the one with the handle hole) slides along a rebate to prevent the concertina folding accidentally. Such slides are frequently fitted with a drawer to take cards, gaming chips, etc.

construction would show, is concealed with a veneer, or else the centre ply is cut away and a stringing line put in its place. The second technique gives considerable strength to such galleries and is a valuable indication that the piece is constructed correctly – that it is genuine, and not copied.

The earliest examples of tea tables and card tables are supported on gate legs. By about 1720 the concertina arrangement was evolved for best quality tables, with a series of hinges enabling the table, when opened, to display a leg at each corner and an apron all the way round. This style had died out by around 1760 and was rarely used again, although I have seen one freak example made of satinwood in about 1790. Most card and tea tables are supported by an arrangement whereby either one or both back legs swing out on a knuckle joint and the top is supported by the upper surface of the legs, sometimes lined with baize. The wood forming the knuckle joint is usually beech and, because this wood is very susceptible to wear and woodworm and because the joint itself is rather unsatisfactory, this part is repaired or replaced frequently. By about 1810,

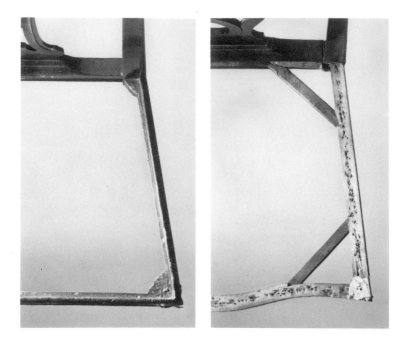

34 *Far left*: A trap-seat chair. Note the rebate in the narrow seat rails, and the small glued blocks flush with the rebate at each angle.

35 *Left*: Beech seat rails for a stuff-over seat. This is slightly unusual in having braces at the back as well. The holes in the seat rails indicate numerous visits to the upholsterer (note also several nail holes in the shoe).

card tables in the Regency style no longer had swinging fly legs and the whole of the frieze remained stationary, while the top pivoted on a joint about two-thirds of the way along its length and folded over the rest of the frieze. These were the only methods of card table support until the 1840s.

With chairs, the seat rails are the most revealing items of construction. There are two ways in which a dining chair may be made. First, it may have a drop-in (or trap) seat, in which case the seat rails will be less than an inch (25 mm) in width and will be rebated to accept the seat. Small blocks will be glued into the corners, giving additional strength to the mortise and tenon joints, but the size of the glued blocks will seldom exceed $\frac{3}{4}$ inch (19 mm) in either direction. Alternatively, the chair may be upholstered by bringing the material down over the seat rail: this is called a stuff-over seat. In this case the chair will have a piece of wood approximately $4\frac{1}{2}$ inches (115 mm) to 6 inches (150 mm) long and $\frac{3}{4}$ inch (19 mm) square rebated into the front and side seat rails. This is known as a corner brace and does not often appear at the rear corners. When upholstered in this way the webbing causes considerable strain on the side rails, which the braces support.

The seat rails in stuff-over chairs are almost always made of beechwood for the simple reason that beech takes upholstery nails very easily, and it is not necessary to replace the seat rails when the chair is re-upholstered. However, beech is highly susceptible to woodworm and it is not uncommon to find an

Regency card table action

eighteenth-century chair which has been re-railed because the original timber had become infested. Braces often drop out when a chair is being upholstered, and it is quite common for an upholsterer to replace them with triangular pieces of wood screwed to the rails. This was a common form of construction in the nineteenth century and might suggest that a chair was made at that time unless one notices marks where braces have once been.

Until the beginning of the nineteenth century, the uprights or stiles on the back of the chair were the one exception to the general rule of furniture that stiles should reach the top. Before this time the top rail of a chair was always mortised and the stiles tenoned into it as was the central splat, which also tenoned into the back seat rail. However, the splat is glued only at the top joint; the bottom end is left floating to allow for shrinkage. The shoe will be rebated to accept the splat, or it may, with a trap seat, be through-tenoned: that is the splat may go right through the shoe, which is glued to back seat rail. With a stuff-over seat the shoe must be removable for the upholstery to pass beneath it. Consequently it is usually tacked on with a nail, and a chair which has been re-upholstered on a number of occasions should have several nail marks where they have been replaced.

With eighteenth-century armchairs, the arms are usually screwed to the seat rails and into the stiles at the back. The screws are countersunk and a small block of wood is used to conceal the hole. If the arm has been strengthened or repaired, this piece of wood will have been removed and since it is made of the same wood as the rest of the chair, the replacement will be obvious. It is impossible to re-use the original piece. Very rarely, the arm is dovetailed rather than screwed into the side seat rail. Stretchers are tenoned into the legs and the outside surface of a stretcher should be flush, or very nearly so, with the outside edge of the leg. Occasionally the stretcher uniting the back legs of a chair is set in slightly from the rear surface. Stretchers may be joined to one another in several ways: sometimes they are rebated, more rarely they are dovetailed or even mitred. In English chairs of the seventeenth century, square stretchers did not run into circular legs, nor did circular stretchers run into square legs, or even into the square sections of turned legs. The same rule applies to stretchers which joined one another.

With both tables and chairs it was sometimes thought decorative to have parts of the leg larger than the rest. For example, Elizabethan tables with bulbous 'cup and cover' legs had a centre section (gadrooned and carved) fatter than the top and bottom. A similar effect is sometimes found in furniture of the 1680s and 1690s: a piece of turning larger than the square piece of wood from which the whole leg is made. In such instances the fatter section is created by gluing four additional pieces of wood on to the square; when dry, the whole piece is put on the lathe and decorated. If this procedure has not been followed the piece must have been made at a later date. The same is true of scroll toes and some turned legs with pad feet (Plate 67). The pad foot often overhangs the outline of the turned leg, despite the fact that the leg tapers towards the ankle. Where the pad foot is broader than the square at the head of the foot, a join should also be visible.

In the cabriole leg, however, the whole was cut from a single piece of wood. As this method was rather extravagant, it was reserved for better quality furniture and, especially in the provinces, furniture was still made with turned legs way into the nineteenth century. The ears (or shoulders as they are sometimes called) on either side of the knee of the cabriole leg are always made separately, and the joint should be clearly visible between leg and ear. This particular part frequently becomes loose and is therefore often replaced; when examining a lowboy, stool, chair, or any object with cabriole legs, one should take care to see that all the ears are original.

Cabriole-leg chairs which were intended to be placed in the centre of a room, say behind a desk, had their back legs carved so that the chair could be viewed from all sides and display an equal degree of quality. Many chairs, however, were designed to be placed around the edge of the room. This is particularly true of the highest quality furniture, which was made for state apartments in large houses, where the most formal arrangements of furniture was obligatory. In such cases the front and sides of the chair will be carved but the back legs will be quite plain.

English furniture is unique in its use of casters. The French produced gilded brass (ormolu) mounts for their furniture, frequently using these as a decorative feature. This was very rare in England, and, apart from the magnificent productions of the expatriates Pierre Langlois and Abraham Roentgen, the sole indigenous exponent was the cabinet-maker John Channon, who moved from Exeter to London in the 1730s and produced some fine examples of ormolu mounted furniture, though perhaps more reminiscent of Teutonic or Scandinavian fashions than of the French. However, the English cabinet-makers did use brass for making casters. Much furniture

Cup and cover leg

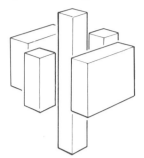

The start

The finish

36 Groups of casters from English furniture. Top row, left to right: modern reproduction with solid brass roller simulating a caster of *c.* 1790. A wooden roller held by iron plate and shackle, *c.* 1730. Brass caster with laminated leather roller, 1775, from the Pembroke table (Plate 97). A large cast brass hairy paw, *c.* 1805. Bottom row, left to right: cast brass caster with circular socket and hollowed roller, *c.* 1800. Cast iron caster with swivelling action of a type fitted to large library chairs and bulky furniture, *c.* 1770. Square box caster with hollowed roller and well shaped shank, *c.* 1790.

produced between 1720 and 1870 had casters fitted, particularly for drawing and reception rooms. Dining chairs were not provided with casters.

The earliest casters were made of wood, frequently laburnum, and were ball-shaped; on large carcase furniture (Plate 85) they were recessed well in from the visible parts of the legs or bracket feet. Most pieces originally fitted with such casters have since had them removed. Laminated leather was the next material used, presumably to keep noise to a minimum, and these rollers were held in a short, brass framework. These early casters were attached to the bottom of the foot or leg by a plate drilled with three countersunk holes, for screw fixing. For lighter pieces, the leather caster continued in use until the 1790s, but the framework was greatly elongated. After this time the roller was almost invariably of brass, but made as light as possible, the inside being cut out; reproductions of this variety usually have solid cylindrical brass rollers which are quite different. At the turn of the century brass casters in the form of a claw or an animal's foot became fashionable.

Around 1775, the square tapered or chamfered leg had given way to the turned leg, which was in widespread use by 1800. The shape of casters had to be changed from the square box and became circular in cross-section: I cannot recall ever having seen a leather roller on such a turned caster. In the nineteenth century legs became fatter and casters followed suit. In mid-century it became customary to make the rollers of white or brown porcelain, which does not wear out so quickly, but on the other hand shatters more easily. Casters of all periods are normally fixed with screws, and the leg is cut in order to accept them. In better designed pieces the caster will be flush with the wood to which it is fitted.

59

Chapter 5
Quality and condition

The quality of a piece of furniture may be considered in three stages. First there is the quality of the design. Even with two chairs taken from the ·same plans, one may be of finer interpretation than the other. Second, there is the quality of materials used; and third, there is the quality of workmanship. By and large these three aspects will complement one another perfectly. For example, the chair illustrated here is supremely

37 Profile of the chair in Plate 72, designed with the human anatomy very much in mind.

38 Plan of the same chair showing the bowed lateral outline.

well designed, anatomically correct and aesthetically very attractive. It is made of the finest timber, with the legs and stiles in straight grained wood which lends strength to the finished article, and the splat has an excellent veneer commensurate with the quality of the design – the very fact that it is veneered indicates a high standard of workmanship.

Quality of workmanship can be assessed fairly easily.

39 Detail of the back of the same chair. Note the straight grain of the stiles, the decorative quality of the splat and the fluency of the carved and shaped decoration.

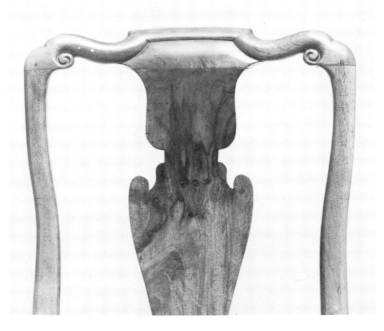

Mouldings, for example, will be complex and crisp in better pieces. Glazing bars in bookcases will be fine and narrow (provided they are made after 1740), and drawer linings will be as thin as the age of the piece permits. In chairs, when viewed from above the back should be bowed to accommodate the round shape of the human back. Similarly, a good quality chair will 'move' when viewed laterally: the back legs should kick down well to give additional stability. In lesser quality chairs, the back may be straight and if the back legs fail to kick out sufficiently the chair will be unstable; consequently the joints are more likely to wear loose.

Quality of design is a more contentious subject. Some people, for example, enthuse wildly over the Regency style of the Brighton Pavilion, while others wax lyrical at the simplicity of early walnut furniture, and others still prefer the Rococo or mother-of-pearl inlaid *papier-mâché* furniture. Yet an experienced observer of old furniture can distinguish a Charles II cane seat-and-back chair from a moderate nineteenth-century copy at a distance. Why exactly the original is thought to be finer in design than the copy lies, I think, outside the scope of this book. That the majority of informed opinion feels this to be the case, however, is quite definite.

In considering quality, it may help to compare the properties of something good, and something *very* good. In Plate 41, the chair on the left is in the French taste, often referred to as French Hepplewhite owing to the fact that George Hepplewhite, in his book of designs, drew a stool and also a console table with legs similar to these. Many people consider that the French Hepplewhite chair represents the pinnacle of achievement in English chair making. There is not a single straight line anywhere in the chair. The design is sound in that such chairs are stable, generally remain in good condition and, despite the fact that they are upholstered in

40 Gadroon mouldings, which only appear on fine quality furniture, require the arts of both cabinet-maker and carver. The lower example shows a typical gadroon mould (from the card table Plate 84), but there is much greater vigour in the upper example, where the crispness of execution displays not only the quality of the original carving, but of the material used.

hard horse hair, are enormously comfortable for very long periods of time.

When I first saw this chair it was still covered in its original upholstery, with brass studs outlining the cartouche shaped back, arm pads and seat rails. The back, too, was originally buttoned in the present manner. Occasionally these chairs have the back outlined in mahogany, but this one, as is often the case, is upholstered all the way round. The arms are shaped to conform in outline with the seat rails, and the upright supports of the arms are carved with moulding and scrolls. The terminals — the end of the arm where one's hand rests — are carved with small garya husks. The arm pads also sit within a raised moulding. The front cabriole legs are carved with a stylised shell upon more garya husks, the ears are in the form of rose paterae and the feet end with a scroll.

The chair on the right, apart from being of generous proportions, is also curvilinear, although the arm terminals are clearly somewhat different. The arm supports are very similar and the legs, while being cabriole, shaped at the knee and ears, are quite plain, but they also terminate in a scroll.

Where then is the difference? The left-hand example is good, as are all French Hepplewhite chairs. They were not the

41 Two mahogany armchairs, c. 1775, inspired by the designs of George Hepplewhite and often described as in the 'French taste'.

product of a second rate chair maker. Yet one must admit that the way the arm sits on its support is somewhat unhappy. The cabriole leg is too narrow at the top, too thin at the ankle and fails to flow as smoothly as it should. The timber is broad-grained, and the chair is somewhat light in weight. The right-hand chair by contrast is very heavy and of fine quality timber. The arm sits delightfully on the upright, which itself is most elegantly curved. The cabriole legs, although plain, are the epitome of fine design and, while the other chair looks as if it might give way under a heavy gentleman, this example will accommodate a heavy man with ease for a great many years. A certain depth of upholstery is necessary and the generous proportions of the seat allow a more satisfying proportion of seat depth to size. The curvature at the back is admirable and gives support where it is most needed. It could be argued that the back would be more elegant if the rear legs had shown above the seat, but despite this one small disadvantage, the right-hand chair is enormously superior to the left, which incidentally is one of a pair.

If the design, materials and workmanship of a piece of furniture are all found satisfactory, the next point to be considered is the condition. Obviously the environment in which it has been kept will determine how often it has been subject to the claws of cats or the devastations of young children. The heavy man who always sits at table on the same chair and is given to leaning back will eventually cause damage. However, a well-made mortise and tenon is very strong indeed and will endure enormous abuse almost indefinitely, and in straight grain wainscot oak or Jamaican mahogany one would be most surprised to see such joints broken. A chair in Honduras mahogany will frequently be considerably eroded on the centre stretcher by wear from shoes and boots, but even moderate San Domingo mahogany will stand the wear of shoes for a very long time.

There is a variety of chair made from about 1770 to 1790 in which the splat is longer than the stiles; it is known as the camel-back chair. The top rail is cut from a piece of wood anything up to five inches wide, and this tends to shrink when exposed to central heating. Consequently the joints loosen and sometimes come apart at the top of the stiles, and breakage frequently occurs at this point. This is an example of how a design can prove faulty in adverse conditions. The camel-back was seldom employed by the finest cabinet-makers, although there are some surprising exceptions to this rule.

There are numerous places to look for wear and tear. Drawer

42 A worn drawer runner. Notice how one section of the drawer runner has eroded completely and how the drawer front has protected the last section.

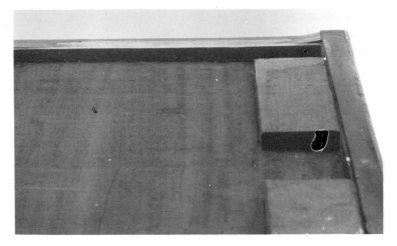

runners in a bureau or chest of drawers will show considerable signs of abrasion, as will the corresponding parts in the carcase. Loop handles, if they are not provided with a back plate, will cause dents in the timber of a drawer front. The human hand leaves traces of dirt and grease in specific places. When a chair is lifted by the person sitting in it, this will occur under the side rails and one should look for signs of dirt at that particular

43 The carcase accommodating the drawer in Plate 42. Notice how the drawer runner has worn grooves at its edge (some of the small marks are caused by grit). The block on the right-hand side mates with a block on the underside of the drawer to prevent it being pushed in too far; this is called a drawer stop.

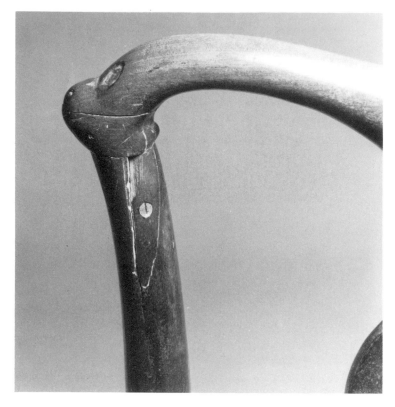

44 The repaired junction of a stile and top rail of a chair. Note the direction of the splits along the grain in both members and the crude screwed repairs. Often new wood has been inserted at this joint.

point. When vacant, chairs are usually lifted by the top rail and similar marks may be found on the underside of that. If the chair is rather heavy it may be dragged rather than lifted, and one should look for wear on the rear edge of the back legs. Chairs are seldom dragged sideways and therefore one would not expect much wear in this direction.

Because the junction between the stile and the top rail of a chair is weak, and because this is a place where a chair is frequently handled, it is also one of the first places to become damaged to such an extent that repair becomes necessary. Similarly, the chair may become so worn on its back legs that some form of restoration is necessary. Other places on a chair where a different type of wear takes place include the joints round the seat rails and on chairs made later than 1720 the glue will loosen and the whole chair becomes wobbly. When this happens it is a perfectly straightforward operation to knock the chair apart, clean up the joints and re-glue them. Sometimes, however, owners do not think of this, or perhaps they have only just re-upholstered the chairs when they notice the rails are loose. Instead of doing the job correctly, they drill a hole and try to hold the joints together with screws. This inevitably leads to a messy area of repair.

Another reason for chairs failing into disrepair is the habit owners have of recovering trap seats without first removing the existing cover. I have even seen trap seats upholstered with as many as six covers, one on top of the other. Each layer of material expands the size of the trap seat, and since the recess into which it is forced remains constant in size, undue strain is placed on the seat rails. Eventually, it only needs the weight of a human to force the seat too far in and breakages occur.

Among the weakest points in a chair are the stiles just above the rear legs, and the very tall chairs of the late seventeenth and very early eighteenth centuries are frequently damaged here. Stretcher rails are often thin pieces of wood, since they are merely braces and are not designed to carry any weight; consequently, they are easily broken. More often than not the whole stretcher is replaced, but they are sometimes repaired if they break where the centre stretcher joins them. When examining a set of chairs the experienced observer will pick up each one in turn and examine the top rail for signs of breakage where the seat meets the back, then check for signs of damage to the seat rails as a result of incorrect upholstery, observe the amount of wear on the rear legs and front leg, and carefully check the stretchers.

Minor damage of this kind may be found in numerous places, so the observer must adopt the attitude of a detective and consider where a piece is most likely to have suffered. If signs of ageing occur in some places but not all, danger signals flash for the experienced observer (Plate 47). For example,

45 The front corner of a trap-seat chair. The seat has been forced outwards by too many new upholstered covers being placed on top of the old worn ones. The breakage caused here is typical.

a knee-hole desk with only the outer edges of each drawer worn would make one suspect that it was once a chest of drawers; the wide drawers down its length may have been cut and a knee-hole inserted. This is a frequent occurrence, and in such cases one looks for lack of wear in the carcase on the inside edges of each small drawer. A skilled mutilator will try to copy accurately the spacing and quality of the dovetails on the inside of each drawer, but is unlikely to have the perfect match of timber. It is equally unlikely that the signs of wear on the drawer runners and in the carcase can be simulated. Finally, the observer should turn the piece of furniture upside down to see that no alterations have taken place structurally.

Clearly furniture like this is unacceptable to the collector and constitutes a composite article. For many years the straight-front chest of drawers was considered unimportant and of little value, while the knee-hole always enjoyed a healthy market. It is little wonder that many generations of cabinet-makers have converted the one into the other. But when does alteration cease to be repair and cause a piece of furniture to jump suddenly into another category? This question has been the subject of countless debates, but current thinking is that repair should be considered acceptable only when occasioned by fair wear and tear. The enhancement of any piece over its original design is unacceptable to the collector, but it will continue to happen so long as a premium is paid for objects of greater utilitarian and aesthetic merit.

It is important to remember that every piece of furniture was once new, and during what we now regard as the period when antiques were made, cabinet-makers had no need to stain any structural member. Wood turns dark naturally through ageing, oxidisation and the gathering of dirt. The lower surface of any piece of furniture, therefore, should only exhibit evidence of this, and any stain on, say, a chair seat rail, should be regarded with suspicion and is probably the result of some later repair, or an indication that the piece was made at a later date. Having said that, it must be remembered that certain specialist techniques, such as lacquering and gilding, do involve the use of stain.

Most tripod tables have a hingeing top (page 39), which made storage easier and allowed the table to double as a firescreen when the top was folded to its vertical position. If the top revolves, it will be supported by a bird-cage arrangement of two blocks secured by four pillars. The column support of the table passes through a hole in the bottom block and is located by a pin between them. Both this type and the non-rotating

46 *Opposite top*: Undersurface of an oval-top stool. The decorative scrolled hole in the top is designed for easy transportation. Compare the accumulation of dirt and the patination at that point and also a comparable surface around the edge of the top. Most particularly, however, note the 'dry' surface inside the apron where the stool cannot be touched with normal usage.

47 *Opposite below*: The underside of the lowboy in Plate 81. Notice the dry, unstained appearance of all the wood, although some dirt has seeped through the planks of the top, and the centre drawer partly removed shows signs of being made of second-hand timber. The drawer runners appear many shades lighter because the timber is newer having been recently abraided. Note the patination and colour of all the surfaces. This is the epitome of an 'honest' piece.

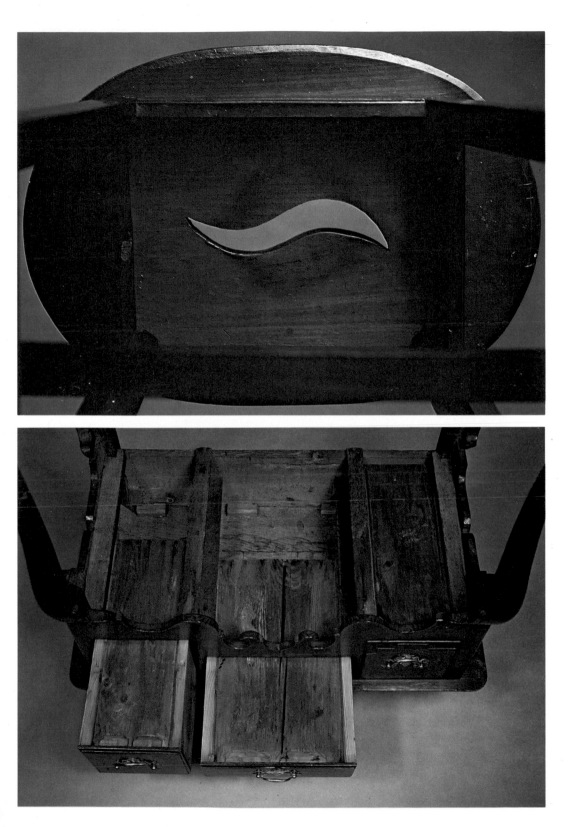

70

49 *Right*: On the left a tripod polescreen of about 1765, carved on the knee and on the vase column. Beside it is a circular tray of about the same date. It is a common malpractice to cut the pole-screen below the banner and to place the tray on top to form a low table.

48 *Opposite*: A fine mahogany tea-kettle stand with a triangular serpentine pie-crust top supported by flying 'C' scrolls. The base includes numerous Rococo carved motifs – claw-and-ball, fish scale, acanthus, gadrooning and beading, and the column is fluted, *c.* 1750. The silver kettle is of comparable quality and was made in London in 1739 by William Kidney.

tripods have some lopers or bearers to support the top, unless it is quite small. The column on the non-rotating table will be tenoned into the block, while with the bird-cage type the column will show through the top block and be wedged into position. Since the top is opened and closed frequently both these methods of fixing leave imprints on the undersurface of the table top. If the top has been altered or replaced or if the lopers have been moved, the presence of a previous arrangement will always show.

The tops of tripod tables often mirrored the contemporary taste in trays and *vice versa*, and this has been a source of much trickery. A few years ago trays had little value, as did pole firescreens, but torchères and carved tripod tables have always been highly esteemed. It was therefore common to take a pole screen, reduce the column in height and fix a tray on the top. The only part which would show as new was the block beneath the tray, but as this was often made with beechwood in

50 The undersurface of a pie-crust tray. Note the considerable abrasion and scratch marks and the complete lack of any fixing showing this has never been a table.

genuine pieces and therefore liable to woodworm, its replacement was not unlikely. To a very experienced eye the design will give the game away, but close examination should reveal the scratch marks which every tray inevitably accumulates on its underside.

Other very popular items for which the demand far exceeds supply include low wine tables and similar objects, made to accommodate tea kettles standing on their original burners, known as kettle stands. Like commodes and console tables, these objects were found only in grand houses and were very rare; moreover they had a limited period of manufacture, from around 1720 to 1770. Here again, pole screens with their upper column cut off were frequently fitted with a small tray. These are often 18-23 inches high (457-584 mm), while original tripod or occasional tables stand 27-30 inches (686-762 mm) high.

From about 1880 to 1925 Sheraton-style furniture, in mahogany with satinwood cross-banding, was much in vogue. Many plain pieces of furniture, which were deemed to have an adequate outline, were insufficiently decorated with inlay to be saleable. A glance through art magazines of the first twenty years of this century will show considerable numbers of inlaid sideboards, chests of drawers, wardrobes and so forth. Many of these we accept today for what they are, genuine late eighteenth-century pieces, inlaid and cross-banded at a later date. Except on the square, tapered legs of card tables and sideboards, boxwood stringing lines were not inlaid into solid timber during the Georgian period (you can check whether the timber is solid or not by looking at the grain on the other side).

It is difficult to set a new stringing line in an old piece without marking the surrounding wood, so when examining cross-banded furniture, careful attention should be given to the timber inside the cross-banding. Look for scratches which stop suddenly at the decoration, for these are either the result of the most amazing coincidence, or more likely, show that the cross-banding was put in at a later date. Bear in mind that timbers used for cross-banding are usually much harder and denser than the ground wood, and so a scratch there may not be as deep. It should also be noted that whole pieces of furniture were sometimes stripped and French polished when this redecoration took place. In such instances much of the beauty will have been lost anyway, but re-polishing, particularly with a dark varnish, always gives grounds for suspicion.

The surface and colour of furniture are themselves important indicators. The first consideration of the polisher is to fill the holes and channels made by the grain. Exactly how furniture was finished in the seventeenth century is uncertain, but oak was polished with waxes of several different varieties, primarily a beeswax softened with a medium to allow an even application. Many people today advocate a simple mixture of beeswax and turpentine, and this recipe has no doubt been in use for a very long time. However, it does leave the surface quite sticky, and impossible to polish without the use of further solvents.

If this mixture was used in the seventeenth and early eighteenth centuries, it would account for the darkening of many pieces of early oak furniture by the accumulation of surface dirt. Indeed, a close inspection of any piece of seventeenth-century furniture will almost certainly reveal black deposits on any surface not easily reached with a polishing duster. On the top of a coffer or chest of drawers, for example, the rear third tends to be darker and dirtier than the front, which is more accessible for polishing and dusting. Exactly how seasoned wood behaves over a very prolonged period is uncertain but, judging from the dirty deposits which often accumulate, one may presume that the grain itself exudes sticky substances which attract dust.

Walnut furniture was polished before it left the workshop.

In order to fill the grain and produce a flat surface on which to build a shine, it seems likely that the timber was painted with several coats of very diluted glue – Scotch glue, made from animal bones, hooves and so forth, which is still used today. After the wood was coated, it was rubbed down to a fine surface and then polished with wax. This process appears to have continued for some time, although exactly what sealing and filling substance was employed after the introduction of mahogany is quite uncertain.

By the 1820s it was realised that timber could be sealed with clear varnish. The application of many coats, and the sanding down of the surface between each coat, is called French polish, and during the nineteenth and twentieth centuries thousands of pieces of furniture have been cleaned and subjected to the French polishing process. This is incompatible with the desires of the collector and accordingly, with more widespread knowledge and appreciation of furniture, many such pieces have been re-cleaned and given a surface which the polisher thinks approximates the old one. French polish or varnish should only be removed by an antique restorer, who may use solvents, methylated spirits or any number of other preparations to make the surface ready for re-waxing.

In an old surface one expects to see a certain degree of scratching, bruising and staining, depending on the use to which the piece has been put. Dining tables are an exception, for they were almost invariably covered with cloths until this side of the First World War and one therefore expects a Georgian dining table to be relatively free of staining. The interior of a bureau, however, would be fairly heavily stained with ink and one should also bear in mind that damp or wet iron, left in contact with wood, produces a black stain in reaction with the tannic acid contained in timber. Before the invention of stainless steel and plastic, many vessels were made of iron and one may reasonably expect to see a number of circular black stains on tables and cupboards.

Most people would prefer an old surface to be free from stains, but where they do occur the owner faces a dilemma, as some colours are considered more desirable than others. Perhaps the best way of deciding is to examine the collections in our museums and stately homes or the stocks of leading dealers, who will always be willing to discuss the colour and surface of any item they have in stock. During the latter half of the nineteenth and the beginning of the twentieth centuries it was customary for dealers themselves to clean oak, and one will sometimes find good quality seventeenth-century oak in exceptionally clean condition which has already acquired quite a good surface. Such pieces may even bear the dealer's trade label.

The balance must be drawn between smartness on the one hand and mellowness on the other. In the late eighteenth century satinwood was sometimes inlaid with purpleheart, boxwood and other timbers, to a most bright and garish effect. A look at any modern reproduction will soon make this clear. Over the years, however, the wood in original pieces has oxidised and the surface has been built up with wax, polish, dirt and more polish, and the end result is a great deal more mellow. If such an object passes into the hands of someone who cares very little, and stores it for example in a damp shed, the glory of its former being soon degenerates into something very shabby. If the piece is then resurrected, the effects of its temporary relegation are only too apparent and the new owner must decide whether the shabbiness is preferable to the original gaudy surface.

Where a surface is simply dirty through grime, a mild kitchen abrasive can be used, though with extreme care. Perhaps a safer method is carefully to apply a cloth moistened with a mixture of turpentine, methylated spirit, vinegar and linseed oil. This will loosen the sort of dirt created by greasy hands and dust, and will leave the surface suitable for wax polishing. It will be noticed that the proprietary brands of furniture polish fall into three categories. Those containing silicones cannot be advised for antique furniture which has not been French polished. Wax should be used instead – either the soft polishes containing a high proportion of aromatic oils and solvents, or the harder polishes generally available only at specialist suppliers. The soft wax polishes, if used regularly, will clean even the dirtiest piece of furniture after a few months and are to be commended for general use. Harder waxes are used in workshops, and restorers and dealers will give advice on their use which is generally confined to building up a surface after stripping.

In the preceding pages of this book, I have explained to the reader the main things he will need to know when looking at a piece of furniture: the names of its constituent parts, the materials from which it is made, the evolution of its design, the way it is put together, and factors affecting its quality and condition. In the next section, all these strands will be drawn together in a series of descriptions of individual items of furniture, taken chronologically.

Part two   Chapter 6
Individual items

We shall start this section of the book with a description of the coffer or chest (or kist, if you live in the North of England) illustrated in Plate 59. It measures 24 inches (610 mm) wide, 20 inches (510 mm) high, and 14 inches (355 mm) deep, and is medieval in form and construction, though it would be an exceedingly rash person who would date such a piece to within even 100 years. The style is perhaps fourteenth century. Such a piece is often referred to in the trade as an ark coffer, because of the canted shape of the top. It is made from oak, riven with a riving iron or froe, and the horizontal members of the lid can be clearly seen to be of long triangular section as one would expect of a split log. All the constituent parts are split and, because the grain of oak is not arrow-straight, the timber undulates along its surface. This is particularly noticeable if one runs one's hand across the surface, and can be seen in the photograph on the rear plank of the top. Save for the cut of the

51 Detail of the end of the coffer in Plate 59 showing its construction.

grooves in the front legs and the cut of each plank to a length, a saw has not been used in its making.

The sides of the coffer simply rest in a rebate in the stiles. The stiles are kept a set distance apart by braces tenoning right through them, and the photograph clearly shows the pegs holding the tenons in place. The tenons, too, can be seen protruding through the front stiles in the photograph. The front board, which accommodates the lock, is tenoned into the stiles. The lid is made of three planks overlapping and rebated into one another, and they in turn are rebated into the thick horizontal members, again each piece being held together with pegs. The hasp is fixed on the inside of the lid, which hinges on pin or peg hinges. The medullary rays or silver fleck can be seen in most sections as the wood was split radially. The colour is pale and faded.

While it is useful to introduce this section of the book with a very early piece of furniture, one should stress that it is most unlikely that any reader would come across a piece of this age outside a museum. Coffers comprise the large proportion of pieces surviving from the medieval period. The more important ecclesiastical counterparts would have been carved with a religious subject enabling one to hazard a reasonable opinion as to the date. But the simplicity of this example, although giving the coffer an enormous amount of appeal, is a stumbling block where accurate dating is concerned.

One of the most prestigious pieces of furniture in the early part of the seventeenth century was the buffet. It was a dual purpose item, often employed for storage, but perhaps its main use was the display of important silver and pewter. Another valuable possession was porcelain from China, and the cupboard illustrated in Plate 52 perhaps originally had a display of blue and white porcelain and silver on the top and on the lower shelf.

The upper section has a pair of cupboard doors flanking a panel, and each door has a central panel framed with stiles and rails which are channel moulded. Each door panel is carved with strap-work and a geometrical arrangement of formal, stylised flowers. The door opens to reveal the cupboard inside, extending behind the central panel, and has a small shelf high up at the back and another shelf behind the overhanging frieze. The central panel between the doors is formed as an arch, with applied mouldings of pieces of wood carved with 'S' scrolls flanking the central arch which is carved with a stylised tree. The Romanesque arch, of which this is an example, was a

veneered form of decoration on more complicated furniture at this time. It is sometimes carved from a single piece of wood in a panel, but where a deeper relief effect is required, as here, the use of applied mouldings is quite correct. Although these pieces are obviously held on with glue we will note that glue is not used structurally.

The locks are no longer present, but one can see rebates on the inside of the door where they were once fitted and this would indicate that the cupboard perhaps held valuables rather than food. The frieze is carved with a band of continual 'S' scrolls with foliate terminals. All this is below the architectural corbels which support the top. The decoration carries on round the side, and the frieze overhangs the cupboard doors by some 5 inches (127 mm) at the front, and is supported by unnecessarily massive turned supports. On marginally earlier examples the pair of cupboard doors would have been canted, that is the cupboard section would have been a half hexagon, whereas earlier still the cupboards would

53 Carved heraldic beast. This diminutive creature measures 3″ high and comes from a piece of furniture dating from 1608. Larger versions appear instead of turned supports on buffets and refectory tables.

54 Detail of the bottom left hand rail. The abrupt halting of the decoration could give ground for suspicion, but closer inspection reveals that it was done deliberately.

have been entirely lacking and the piece would have been three shelves. The retention of the supports on the top is therefore quite understandable, if by this time superfluous. Soon afterwards these were done away with, and in eighteenth century examples (mainly from Wales) a pendant turning is considered sufficient decoration (see Plate 58).

Below the waist shelf is a convex moulding above a band of strap-work, part of which forms the drawer illustrated in Plate 25a. The construction of the drawer is fully illustrated in the chapter on drawers. Below all this lies the bottom shelf, set on another band of carving of alternate lunettes and inverted lunettes. The bun feet below that are not original, although they probably date from the latter end of the seventeenth century.

Many variations exist on this theme. Very rarely pieces such as this may have had an additional shelf. Fine sixteenth-century examples have, instead of turned supports, carved heraldic beasts, and sometimes the carving is substituted with geometrical inlays. Because buffets were always considered prestigious, they have always been much in demand. Consequently there are in existence plain cupboards which have been carved in the nineteenth century, and many more examples which are completely made at that time in the style of the seventeenth century.

It has been stated elsewhere that it is very difficult to make firm assertions or rules about furniture making, and this is clearly demonstrated by the bottom rail of this example. The bench in Plate 62 has a similar lunette carving, the design of

which ends at a logical point at its junction with a stile. The reader would be well advised to reserve judgment therefore about the bottom rail of this example, where a half round is cut abruptly in the middle. Very close examination will reveal, however, that although the decoration terminates in this way it is almost certainly deliberate.

The cupboard or wardrobe illustrated in Plate 55 apparently dates from the first half of the seventeenth century – but does it? The lunette carvings on the top rail of the doors are typical of that period and bear close resemblance to the carvings on the bench (Plate 62) and the buffet (Plate 52). The moulded stiles and rails are equally right for that date, as are the surface and colour. Cupboards of this size and shape were not unknown in the period – but that is as far as the 'rightness' of this piece goes. In fact, it is of twentieth-century manufacture, but constructed of carved room panelling made in the seventeenth century.

The top rail above the doors is carved in such a way that the design finishes correctly at each end, but the top rail of the left-hand door finishes in mid-lunette, and the decoration is in a different design altogether. Seventeenth-century pegs, when they have not been moved, present a very clean edge and almost invariably stand slightly proud of the surrounding surface. Those in the present example have been bashed and hidden and clearly are not original. The centre stile, between the doors, is not even pegged into the top rail, and no seventeenth-century joiner would have made such an omission.

On opening the door, further signs of this lack of authenticity are abundantly clear. The whole of the back is modern stained pine with machine planing marks and, while the base is old, the top has been reconstructed, as have the back, sides and rails. The side panels one would expect to be of equal size, but the top is very weak, and no seventeenth-century joiner would have finished a piece without a cornice complementing the shape and size of the article he was making. Had there ever been one, signs of its fixing would be evident.

For all that, the cupboard is very practical and fits in well with furniture contemporary to the date of its panels. The hinges, while of almost correct design and fixed with hand-wrought nails, are impressed with a nineteenth-century maker's stamp. Pieces like this abound in antique shops and auction rooms. To many people they have the attraction of being both functional and a great deal less expensive than the

55 An oak cupboard or wardrobe, constructed from seventeenth-century room panelling.

real thing. Constructed in the present form the piece was clearly not intended to deceive. The maker constructed a wardrobe to use up some seventeenth-century panelling at his disposal, and this is therefore a composite piece of furniture. Its value is merely that of a practical article, not of an antique, but I think many people would prefer this to a nineteenth-century oak cupboard carved in much the same style.

The court cupboard illustrated in Plate 60, dating from *c.* 1640, is a delightful example because its condition is exemplary, it is unusually small and the carving is both crisp and varied. These attributes weigh heavily in its favour, but it cannot be said to be exceedingly fine because it is neither inlaid nor carved with fabulous beasts – this is perhaps the distinction between something which is eminently collectable and the superlative pieces to be found in our museums.

The top overhangs the upper section and is carved with 'S' scrolls which terminate in a leafy motif. The columns, which in earlier examples would have supported the overhanging top, have now been reduced to a pendant turning, and the upper section is merely a cupboard with one opening door in the centre, flanked by a pair of panels which do not open. The stiles and muntins are carved in exactly the same fashion as the top rail, while the other rails have a simple punched arched motif of small size. The carved panels on either side are in the form of a Norman arch, enclosing a stylised tree. The central door is similarly decorated, but the mitred framing is plain and accommodates the small decorated strap hinges. Below the waist ledge is a rail of fluted decoration, while the stiles, other rails, and muntins are decorated with gouged channel moulding with an arrangement of carved panels flanking the plain door.

The simple carving below is a combination of geometrical and stylised leafy motifs, while the members forming the central cupboard door are plain channel moulded. The hinges are all of the bifurcated strap type, often reproduced at a later date, although these examples are original. The heart-shaped iron handles may once have been elsewhere, but are probably original to the piece. The whole construction is, as one would expect, mortised and tenoned and double pegged. The end panels are quite plain, though the rails are channel moulded like the lower cupboard door. The surface is quite original, though fairly dark, and the timber is oak throughout. Much of the desirability of this piece derives from its very small size: only $50\frac{1}{2}$ inches (1280 mm) wide by 49 inches (1245 mm) high by 17 inches (432 mm) deep. As with all court cupboards, the inside is floored with boards some $\frac{3}{8}$ inch (9.5 mm) thick running from back to front. It would be most unusual in a piece of this age to come across any other form of construction.

The coffer illustrated in Plate 56 is a good seventeenth-century example. At this time there was a definite pecking order for the decoration of coffers. The first member to receive attention would be the top rail and the front panels would normally be next, although occasionally the stiles and muntin(s) would be

56 A small carved, panelled, oak coffer dating from the latter end of the first half of the seventeenth century.

decorated while the panels remained plain. Finally the joiner might decorate the side panels in the same order, rail first and then panel. The tops were never more than moulded in any coffer and carving here should be regarded with considerable suspicion.

In the present example the front top rail is carved with the same configuration of lunettes and stylised foliage as the bench in Plate 62 and the cupboard in Plate 55. It is perhaps the most common of all seventeenth-century decoration, but it would be well to note the depth and fineness of the carving and the fact that the colour in the decoration is the same as on the top surface. The panels are carved with stylised tulips, although the foliage is hardly that of a bulb. The tulip was a Stuart emblem and was most common in carved furniture of the period, as well as being found in other forms of decoration such as brass, silver and pottery. The stiles and bottom rail have a rebated channel mould with a slight, incised diaper motif. Very frequently such mouldings would be elaborated with punched star decoration or dots between the crosses, but the present example is plain. The rails are channel moulded, but it will be noticed that the moulding peters out before the central muntin: this is quite common on genuine pieces but seldom appears on reproductions. The side panels on the present example are plain, only the top rail being moulded on its lower edge. The top is equally plain and made from two panels – such

57 The back of a candle box displaying several forms of punched decoration. The front of the box is carved.

pieces have from two to six panels forming the top (though three or four is the norm). In this instance the muntins are moulded, while the rails are chamfered on their inside edges. The back has a single panel running the entire length of the coffer, which is somewhat unusual, and retains its original wire hinges. These can be seen where they protrude through the lid.

Mention has been made of punched decoration. Carving was the most common form of decoration during the age of oak, although inlay was used during the sixteenth century and for the first few years of the seventeenth. Where small designs were required to run along a stile or rail, punched decoration was often employed. A tool was fashioned by the joiner or his blacksmith with a star, crescent, circle, dot or cross, usually of approximately $\frac{1}{4}$ inch (6 mm) in diameter. This tool was struck with a mallet and left its impression along a line as a shallow decoration.

Almost coinciding with Queen Victoria's accession to the throne in 1837 came a revival of the Gothic – for example, Barry and Pugin started to build the Houses of Parliament in 1840. Gothic designs had been revived before, in the 1760s and again in the 1800s, but this latest fashion went to much greater lengths to copy the feeling of the Gothic than the mere adaptation of certain motifs. The fashion blossomed and soon encompassed all forms of medieval, Tudor, renaissance and other early art forms. Anything of oak, carved and purporting to be pre-1700, whether real or genuine, was much esteemed. A great many pieces of furniture were made reproducing earlier styles, while a large quantity of early furniture was redecorated. During the first half of the seventeenth century and later in country areas, a considerable amount of oak furniture had been made which was very plain. In the nineteenth century much of this earlier furniture was 'improved' by carving the panels to sixteenth and seventeenth century patterns. Sometimes the decoration was overtly alteration, on other occasions it was intended to deceive.

The cupboard illustrated in Plate 58 is just such a piece. The

58 Court cupboard dated 1670, but made perhaps as much as 200 years later incorporating earlier sections.

lower half is a simple seventeenth-century cupboard and the channel moulding and gouged decoration are as honest as any set of stiles and rails could be. The panels are also seventeenth century, but their decoration is not. The upper section, carved with dragons which appear to have squirrels' tails, is entirely nineteenth century and largely a pastiche of Victorian ideas of what seventeenth-century furniture should look like. A comparison of the stylised foliage and lozenge carving with genuine pieces is worthwhile, for the difference is difficult to describe in words, and the reader is urged to try to find some examples and make a careful examination. The use of split balusters is slightly incorrect, as they were in fashion in the 1670s whereas the lozenge and foliage decoration is more common on earlier pieces, and it is unusual to have the two forms of decoration in one piece. The addition of snakes is completely wrong and gives the first indication that the whole piece is a fake. The carving of the date, 1670, and the initials A.C. indicates that the piece was intended to deceive when it was made, and it is interesting to note that the lettering of the initials is quite inconceivable for that date.

The amount of information available to the Victorian public was more limited than today, and early reference books show many pieces like this as being genuine. We are fortunate that a great deal more is known today about design and construction than was then and there are very few, if any, knowledgeable people who would now be taken in by this piece. Apart from the actual design, new wood has had to be employed in the construction of the upper section, and this has been stained in order to simulate the colour of the old wood of the lower section. On places where the wood has been handled the stain has rubbed away to reveal much light timber, yet if it had been old wood one would have expected these places to be darker. It is quite impossible to impregnate stain into the wood in such a way that it simulates in depth the colour accumulated by naturally aged wood.

Academics and dealers often dismiss furniture like this as being fake and unworthy of discussion or merit. Yet many thousands of such pieces exist and are for the most part, like this example, wonderfully practical and superbly made. For furnishing a home these items have the added advantage of being inexpensive. The present example is a much treasured family possession, and rightly so. It should not be thought that the analysis above constitutes in any way a denigration; it is merely observing what the article is, and putting its production in a historical context.

59 A riven oak chest, or ark coffer, of medieval construction.

60 Small oak court cupboard, c. 1640, with interesting decoration.

62 *Above*: Oak bench, c. 1640. The sides have lunette decoration and an unusual 'H' stretcher arrangement.

61 *Opposite*: Walnut marquetry escritoire, c. 1690, of high quality and showing continental influence on an English design. The large brass escutcheons are original. The handles are substitutes.

Until 1640 or thereabouts only very important people sat at a meal on chairs; for the most part seating consisted of stools and benches. The bench illustrated in Plate 62 is a typical example dating from the second quarter of the seventeenth century. The top has a simple thumb moulding running round the edge and is fixed to the frieze with pegs at intervals of about 18 inches (457 mm). The top is cut from quartered oak and has occasional black circular marks caused by wet iron containers being placed upon it. The frieze is carved on all sides with lunettes, a motif which was most common in the second quarter of the seventeenth century. It will be noticed that the carving finishes at each end in a logical fashion and was definitely not cut from a longer piece.

The table for which this bench was made was no doubt carved in exactly the same way. However, despite the fact that the bench is carved on all four sides, it would depend upon its original position whether the table would have been carved on one, three, or all four sides. If the table originally sat in the centre of the room it would have been carved on all four sides, but if made to sit along the side of a room, it would have been carved on one side, and possibly on both ends as well, but not on the side nearest the wall. The wall might have been fitted with a built-in bench, but otherwise the present example would have had the pair to match it on the other side of the table. The table for which this was made was perhaps 18 inches (457 mm) longer than this bench, but it could have been considerably larger if a number of matching benches were used

on each side, for example down the centre of a hall. Very often tables were made for stools as opposed to benches, and sets of up to six or more are known, although it is most uncommon to find sets still in existence.

The turnings forming the legs or stiles of this bench would be diminutive interpretations of the larger legs of the corresponding table, and it can be clearly seen that this turning bears a strong resemblance in feel and proportion to the massive turnings of the buffet illustrated in Plate 52. Most commonly the legs of benches are united by four stretchers, running between each leg. It is most uncommon to find an H stretcher as in the present example, but almost certainly this reflected the style of the table to which it belonged. As one would expect every joint is a pegged mortise and tenon. On examination of the inside surface of the frieze, there is a delightful dryness to the timber which has never been polished and acquired only a surface of dust. Examination there also reveals the pegs showing through in every instance. Perhaps the clearest distinction between a reproduction and an old joint stool or bench can be found in the way the holes were drilled for the pegs. If they are drilled right through and the pegs are visible from the inside of the frieze, then they are constructed in the right way – reproductions are frequently not pegged at all or, if pegged, not right through.

On the end surface of the frieze there is a certain amount of

63 The inside undersurface of a joynt stool. Note the protruding pegs and the difference between the surfaces hands can and cannot reach.

shine, but the surface on the outside top of the frieze is quite shiny although dirty and this is due to an accumulation of dirt and grease where the bench has been handled over the years. The undersurface of the centre stretcher rail betrays clearly the marks of the pit-saw and it is perfectly reasonable that this part should not have been finished. The patination of this bench is exemplary and the only drawback is the lack of turning below the level of the stretchers. Originally there would have been one more turning below the stretcher – a diminutive bun foot. It often happened that furniture of this type originally stood on flagstone floors, with the attendant problem of rising damp. No timber will survive this treatment for long and the estate carpenter was called in periodically to trim each foot so that the bench did not wobble as a result of one foot or more being rotted away.

It was stated earlier that it is more common to find stools than benches. Because such pieces were made by a joiner they are known as joyned or joynt stools, but their construction is identical to that of this bench. They are, however, sometimes called coffin stools. This derives from the practice of resting a coffin on such stools in churches at funerals. But it is more pleasant, and certainly correct, to call them joyned or joynt.

Because of their height and small size joynt stools have for many years been a favourite with collectors and people wishing to furnish their houses. There are few good ones left on the market, and it is common to find that one or more stretchers have been replaced, and that the bun feet are no longer present or have been cut off and replaced. They were always held with six pegs securing the top to the rails, but West Country-made ones had tops held into the stiles with four pegs, but this is an unsatisfactory method of fixing as the shrinkage in the top and the leg will be the same. Once the top becomes loose it will soon become separated from the base and will be subject to considerable damage, if not total loss. The tops were always moulded and are most difficult to fake. Comparison with the surface of each side will soon betray signs of a top having been made at a later date. Even when the frieze was completely plain, it was always moulded on the lower edge. Invariably the legs taper outwards when viewed from the end – that is, the base is wider than the frieze – but viewed from the longer side, the legs will be parallel. Conformity of design and size is truly remarkable, and perhaps some scholar will one day write a thesis on how it came about that joynt stools, whether they were made in Northumberland or Sussex, East Anglia or Cornwall, seem always to be of the same configuration.

Just as the bed was the prime status symbol of the house, the babies of wealthy families were accorded quality furniture in the form of cradles. As with any other piece of furniture of this date, the example shown is of panelled construction, and each panel is carved with a lozenge which incorporates many familiar geometrical motifs and 'S' scrolls. The stiles, rails and muntins are pegged, as one would expect, and the head rail at the back is initialled I.L. and dated 1651. It is thought that many of these cradles had rockers, which could be removed so that the cradle would remain stable when required. A plank of wood could then be inserted between the two wings of the cradle to form a seat. By substituting the seat plank with another piece with a hole cut in it, and placing a chamber pot beneath, the cradle became a miniature commode. The purpose of the trap door now becomes apparent!

The finials at the top of the stiles at the head end show where a lathe was used to turn them, and are of very truncated form. Those at the foot are longer but crude and were for holding the cradle in order to rock it. The base boards are all loose, allowing them to be removed for cleaning. It is most rare for the rockers to be original and indeed the present example has replacements, although at first one might be forgiven for thinking them original. Certainly the colour and type of wood is comparable to the rest of the piece; however, at the tail end the

64 Oak cradle dated 1651, with panels of lozenge carving.

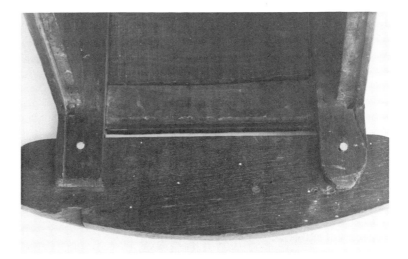

upper edges are almost razor sharp and there is no edge in the rest of the piece which bears comparison to this sharpness.

On careful examination the rocker reveals marks at the head where handles have once been, indicating without doubt that this piece of wood was once a drawer front. This does not in itself make the rocker not genuine, as it is known, particularly in the seventeenth century, for joiners to use second-hand timber for making a piece. The mark left by the handle, however, is of the type not used before about 1750 – a hundred years after the cradle purports to have been made – and it is for this reason that one must doubt the rocker's authenticity. The condition of the cradle leaves something to be desired. The colour is rather grey and uninteresting, and the carving is not of enormously high quality. Comparison of the depth and crispness of the carving with that of the buffet illustrated in Plate 52 will leave no doubt about the bold and surehanded carving of a superior craftsman on the buffet – on the cradle the execution is weak and hesitant. The channel moulding on the rails is good, but the feel of the whole piece suggests it was country-made, with no pretention to great quality. Nevertheless the rarity of furniture of this quality and of this date is sufficient to make it a very desirable piece and much sought after by collectors. It is amusing that today cradles are most frequently used as containers for flower arrangements.

The side-table illustrated in Plate 66 measures $26\frac{3}{4}$ inches (670 mm) wide by $19\frac{3}{4}$ inches (490 mm) deep by $26\frac{1}{2}$ inches (670 mm) high. It dates from 1685-90 and is typical of that period in being 'over-hatted' – the top is considerably larger than the framework below. The top, of quarter sawn oak, shows silver

fleck or medullary rays and is in two planks. The ends have been cleated in order to show long grain along each side and, as befits an article of sophisticated design and workmanship, the cleats are mitred at the corners. This has resulted in the two planks parting company because of shrinkage, despite the fact that the timber was obviously well seasoned. The top also has a half-round moulding to the edge.

The frieze is fitted with a single drawer, the linings of which are thick and very crudely dovetailed. The bottom of the drawer is made of two planks with the grain running from back to front. The drawer front is a single piece of unadorned oak and retains its original gilt-brass, bifurcated drop handles, attached to the drawer with snapes — brass strips which pass through the drawers and divide in the manner of a split or cotter pin. The lock is missing and the present escutcheon is a Victorian replacement: the dirt mark left around the original escutcheon shows quite clearly.

Below the drawer and running around the frieze is a large astragal mould and the supports are barley-twist columns above vase-shaped turnings. These are good examples of the later barley-twist; ten to fifteen years earlier perhaps, they would have been thicker and with a less extended spiral. The stretcher joining the legs is of fretted curvilinear outline and is mitred at the corners. The table rests on diminutive bun feet.

The cabinet-making and the design are quite sophisticated and, when made, this piece was very much in fashion. At this date, however, quality tables were usually finished with floral or seaweed marquetry and *en suite* with a looking glass and a pair of torchères. The stretcher joining the four legs was often in the form of an elaborate cross.

Despite the replacement of one rear bun foot and the lack of the lock and its escutcheon, this table is in a remarkable state of preservation. The surface has never been scraped or re-polished, and has a fine patination.

One remarkable feature is its size, for the vast majority of tables of this design tend to be approximately one quarter as large again or bigger. This was one of the most fashionable ideas imported from France. A grand house would have an enfilade of rooms, each joining the next, and normally with two windows to each room. Between each pair of windows in the first three rooms, which were large, would be a pier, where it would be customary to have just such a table, probably in marquetry, the style closely resembling the escritoire in Plate 61. A pair of torchères would be made in precisely the same way and a mirror, in the form of a simple rectangular plate surrounded by a large convex moulding surmounted by a cresting would be hung above the table.

Up to the sixteenth century, dining tables were of the refectory type – long and narrow; the sophisticated variation on this theme was the draw-leaf table, in which the length was almost doubled by pulling two half flaps underneath each end. By the seventeenth century, eating had become a more private activity and a form of table evolved to suit a family, called the gate-leg table. This is oval, or sometimes circular, and supported on a framework of eight legs. The four immovable legs stand at each corner, while the others are formed in two pairs, each on a separate framework, and pivoting like gates between the stationary legs. The whole

structure is joined by a frieze beneath the top and a stretcher arrangement a short way off the ground.

The earliest of these tables dates from the first quarter of the seventeenth century and is of massive proportions. Occasionally the gate is part of the end legs, in which case the end leg splits in half down its length; this feature is more common on Dutch pieces and is called a split baluster gateleg. A particularly delightful type is that in which the members are made up of spiral twists (sometimes called barley twists) like the table in Plate 66. Almost invariably the uprights are turned, but it is very common for the horizontal members to be of square section and simply moulded, as in the present example, illustrated in Plate 67. The most common sizes for such tables are between 42 inches (1065 mm) and 54 inches (1370 mm), and the present example measures 48 inches (1220 mm) by 56 inches (1420 mm) when extended. It dates from the 1690s. The top has a thumb moulding at the edge and a similar moulding runs along the rule joints where the flaps meet the 'bed', the part of the top which does not hinge. The thicker the top in early gate-legs, the greater the esteem in which they are held today.

67 Unusually elegant gate-leg table of walnut with turned supports and rare carved decoration and 'Spanish' scroll feet, *c.* 1690.

The uprights are turned and tapered, while the frieze is shaped at each end and contains one drawer. The unusual features of the table illustrated are the carved shaped panels where the legs meet the stretchers, and the Spanish scroll feet. These overhang the square section of the main body of the leg, and careful examination of the scroll feet will reveal joints where additional timber has been added. The table is constructed entirely in solid walnut of a somewhat reddish hue, with the exception of the cedarwood frieze at each end. That the cedarwood is original is without doubt because the pegs holding it in position are undisturbed and original. The majority of gate-leg tables one sees on the market today are of oak, and country made. For one to be carved in walnut is an immediate indication of superior quality. That the feet have not worn down, nor been the subject of repair, is both unusual and very desirable.

Unfortunately one leaf has been the subject of more than fair wear and tear and a strip of wood some $4\frac{1}{2}$ inches (114 mm) wide has had to be replaced. It is difficult to imagine why such a large piece of timber has had to be set into a table of this quality. Very often with gate-legs the tip of a flap becomes lost or broken, but for a piece of wood to have to be placed within the flap is almost unaccountable. It is interesting to note that when the restorer inset this piece, he had to clean the surface of the surrounding timber, and coloured the new wood in order to make it match. The restoration is no doubt a great deal more obvious now than it was when it was done, as the colour so applied has since faded, but the rest of the top, with its original surface, has retained its colour. Quite how some former owner managed to lose the drawer also seems inexplicable, but is indeed the case, for the existing drawer is quite new. Closer inspection reveals the application of stain to the wainscot oak, which gives the game away, and the suspicion is confirmed by both the crispness of the edges and the dissimilarity of the wood in the drawer front to that in the rest of the table. One would also expect the top of the drawer linings to be rounded, but they are quite square.

On tables of this nature the most frequent place to find signs of wear and tear is on the edges of the rule joints. When the flaps are in the down position, a gap will appear on the end of the join. When walking past a folded table it is easy for clothing to catch in this tapered gap, and consequently the timber may be subjected to strain and eventually split. Dealers tend to regard tops without any splits in this particular place as an unexpected bonus. Of the four corners on the present example, three have been patched, which is about par for the course.

The reader might well wonder why such a table, with all its faults, has been thought fit to be illustrated. The answer is that it is very rare to find furniture in a completely unrestored state *and* not requiring restoration. The finer the piece of furniture the more rare this is likely to be. In this particular case, the restorer has fortunately not tried to 'improve' upon the original design, but a table with half a flap missing and with a cubby hole where a drawer should be, would clearly have been both useless and ugly. The restoration effected on this gate-leg might well go unnoticed by many people, even in a good light. In bad light they might not be noticed even by an expert.

After the Civil War and the early years of the Restoration of the monarchy in the 1660s, two socially important developments took place. The first was the establishment of a form of postal system on a national scale, with a consequent increase in the number of letters written. The second was the building of a great many fine houses. These concurrent developments resulted in a piece of furniture known as a scriptor, which was also referred to by the French term escritoire. In its simplest form this item had a large panel which could be let down in the front and, when opened, rested horizontally, providing a surface upon which to write, and inside were numerous compartments, and pigeon holes in which to store correspondence, household accounts, bills and so on. Earlier ones were often on a stand, perhaps containing one drawer, and were either made of oak, or, in the case of the more elaborate items, were veneered with kingwood oyster veneers. Later ones employed the full range of decorative detail available at the time. The Huguenot immigration brought with it many techniques of which marquetry had perhaps the greatest influence in furniture decoration (Plate 61).

Cushion drawer construction

68 Detail of the end panel of the escritoire (Plate 61), showing the panel containing marquetry. The cross banding is outlined with light and dark stringing.

The configuration of this escritoire is standard; the cornice is a typical arrangement of complex cross-grain mouldings and immediately beneath is a cushion-shaped moulding which, as was customary, forms a drawer. The cushion moulding extends round the side as well as the front of the piece, and therefore the drawer linings are set well back from the edge of the drawer front. The large panel in the front folds down to reveal a symmetrical arrangement of smaller drawers, pigeon holes and a cupboard. Often the cupboard inside opens to reveal a further arrangement of drawers, and it is not uncommon to find a great many secret drawers in a piece of furniture of this type. The let-down front is secured in its opened or writing position by a folding iron stay which is bolted right through the carcase, and is inset with a leather writing surface within a very broad cross-band. The lock is not square, but rectangular, and, in common with good quality locks of that time (and indeed during the next sixty years), has four shoots when activated. Each section of the side is inlaid with an arch, a common feature, but the depiction of a Roman soldier is more unusual. The cross-banding on the ends is very broad and is further outlined with a black and white stringing. The lower section of this piece is a typical arrangement of two short and two long graduated drawers upon an ogee base-mould, and ebonised bun feet. The carcase has a half round moulding of cross-grain timber separating the drawers. The arrangement of marquetry panels is quite typical, indeed it would be most unusual to find panels inlaid in any other form.

Since very similar marquetry flowers to those shown here can be found on furniture of a very diverse nature – clocks, chests of drawers, cabinets, tables, torchères, mirrors, barometers and many more – it is possible that manufacturers sold this in ready-made panels so that the veneer layer could use them at his own discretion. One might also speculate that outworkers of the marquetry cutting trade were able to produce single flowers and leaves and that the marquetry seller assembled these flowers into the design that we see. Carnations, peonies and tulips appear to be the favoured flowers and acanthus leaves feature prominently too. Some marquetry includes ivory, both of a natural colour and stained green. However, the workings of the marquetry cutting industry are comparatively undocumented and would benefit from more research.

Chests of drawers were first made in England in the middle of the seventeenth century. Early examples had the familiar decoration of the period, namely mouldings arranged geometrically applied to the fronts of the drawers, and the second drawer from the top was quite deep, usually between 9 inches (228 mm) and 11 inches (279 mm). The drawers below this were usually enclosed by cupboard doors. By 1670 the doors were omitted, leaving all the drawers exposed.

The first departure from geometrical mouldings came with the use of veneers. Before exotic foreign timbers were used to any great extent, native laburnum and walnut was cut into 'oysters' and veneered as is shown on the chest of drawers of *c.* 1690 in Plate 69. These 'oysters' were taken from the cross-sections of relatively small limbs on the tree. At the same time it was discovered that a pleasing arrangement was achieved by putting the deepest drawer at the bottom and making each drawer upwards progressively shallower. This arrangement has been in continuous use in all better quality pieces until the present time.

To offset the 'oysters', the present example has been outlined with a cross-banding of pear wood on both the drawer

69 Oyster veneered chest of drawers, *c.* 1690, with geometric inlaid top and bun feet. The handles are replacements of *c.* 1770.

fronts and the sides. The ground wood throughout the carcase is pine. On the top the 'oyster' veneers and pear wood have been arranged in a geometrical pattern based on circles in a way that was very typical of the last fifteen years before 1700. In a better-quality piece, parts of the top might have been filled with marquetry of flowers and foliage, and the sides might have been similarly decorated and with pear wood stringing. The drawer fronts might also have had pear wood stringing or panels of marquetry to emphasise the 'oyster' veneers. The marquetry escritoire (Plate 61) shows this form of decoration, as well as marquetry panels at the side and on the drawer fronts. The similarity of thickness and drawer divides and the use of half round mouldings indicate a very similar date, but while the chest is of very good quality the escritoire is superb.

The broad quarter-round moulding of the chest's top and base has a cross-grain veneer as do the half round mouldings between the drawers. These features are common to many pieces of this quality, whether they are chests of drawers, wardrobes, knee-hole desks or any other carcase furniture. The drawer bottoms are rebated into the sides and front, and the drawers slide on the whole bottom surface; the amount of wear is minimal as the load has been spread over a wide area. The drawer linings are held to the front by coarse dovetails

101

running right to the front of the drawer, which are only hidden by the veneer (Plate 25b).

The handles are of good quality, but date from about 1770 and are merely replacements. The original handles were fixed where the inside pommel is now and they probably resembled the bifurcated drops illustrated in Plate 66. The top drawers were probably opened with a key only; the escutcheons would have been of cartouche shape, and probably engraved. The replacement escutcheons, though possibly dating from 1740, are more likely contemporary with the existing handles as they are of a design which remained in fashion for many years, indeed well into the nineteenth century. The elm bun feet, although old, are possibly not original, though perfectly in keeping with the design of the rest of the piece.

This chest of drawers represents the earliest type made in the same way as they are today – a break from the pegged stile and rail type with geometrical mouldings. It is also a very early example of the use of veneers, which indicate a craftsman working to the latest dictates of fashion. The inclusion of oyster veneers gives one the first and strongest indication of date, which is confirmed by the mouldings, timbers and construction of the carcase and drawers. The chest fulfils its utilitarian function as well today as it did when it was made and is of high, though not supreme, quality.

The chair illustrated in Plate 77 is one of a set of six. They date from about 1710 and are made of walnut, beechwood and pine. However the entire visible framework is lacquered red. The back is brilliantly coloured and embossed leather and the top rail is a shaped arch with a foliate cresting centred by a curious double cartouche. The top rail, stiles and bottom rail are all vigorously moulded with complex astragal, part of which forms the moulding which runs around the seat rails. Below the back is a pendant of carved foliage, hatching, and an inverted shell. The seat is also decorated like the back. The cabriole front legs are boldly curved with no loss of proportion for their vigour. (It is so easy for a cabinet-maker to go a little too far in the curve of the cabriole leg which then immediately loses all its appeal.) The upper sections of the cabriole are outlined with a moulded 'C' scroll, the feet are perfectly plain and pad-shaped. The back legs have a turned section above the square bottom member which kicks out in a most pronounced fashion, as one would expect of a fine quality chair. The stretcher arrangement is shaped and moulded whereas the one uniting the rear legs is simply turned.

Several points are of interest here. Such chairs are part of the important furnishings of a state room. Embossed leather, often of Spanish origin, was much sought after and highly prized, and the embossing bears a close resemblance to the decoration of silver of that time and its use as the upholstery on furniture is most rare. The framework of lacquer (a most fashionable and expensive decoration) together with the size and proportions of these chairs indicates their importance. The comparison between these and the walnut chair illustrated in Plate 72 with its veneered back, carved knee and stretchers is most interesting. One forms part of an important set of state furniture, the other is delicate and restrained in design although superbly carved and of fine quality.

This is not a judgment of monetary value, but it does point to the difference between finely crafted domestic furniture and important state items such as the one shown here.

The upper section of the bookcase illustrated in Plate 70 has a shaped mirror door flanked with a pair of pilasters, the heads of which are carved with acanthus, egg-and-dart, and scrolls – an elaborate variation on the Ionic column. The mirror plate has a border of contrasting feather banding and the cornice has a simple cavetto moulding. The door opens to reveal two bookshelves which are adjustable. The lower section has a fall outlined with a double half-round moulding. The centre of the fall is quarter-veneered and is cross-banded and feather banded; it also has a moulding to support a book along its lower edge. It opens to reveal a stepped interior and a recess or well below the writing surface. A pair of lopers support the fall, and below them is a waist moulding. The carcase contains two short and two long graduated drawers outlined by a double half-round moulding on the carcase. The drawers are further outlined with herringbone inlay, and the handles are the engraved plate type with matching escutcheons. The whole piece sits on bun feet beneath a moulding. So far, one might well imagine from the illustration and description that it dates from about 1710, but let us examine the construction in detail.

First, it is correct for the looking-glass plate to be bevelled, but the angle of the bevel is too great. One should scarcely be able to feel a bevel on early eighteenth-century glass. The star cut in the middle of the glass is not quite correct in style for this period, though the idea is right. Also, on putting one's finger nail to the surface of the mirror, the reflection is a full $\frac{1}{4}$ inch (6 mm) from the object, indicating plate glass at least $\frac{1}{8}$ inch (3 mm) thick, too much for a Queen Anne mirror. Looking inside, the

70 A burr ash and walnut bureau bookcase of early eighteenth-century design.

construction is largely correct, but the piece of wood which secures the mirror in place is held with machine-made screws, not hand-made like those of the eighteenth century. The lock is quite original to the door and is stamped 'improved four lever' and is also held with machine-made screws — all decidedly twentieth century!

The inclusion in the design of a bookrest on the fall indicates careful attention to a design of about 1700, but on a genuine piece the cross-banding and the feather banding inside it would be shaped to follow the outline of the bookrest. The lock on the fall of an eighteenth-century bureau seldom measures less than $3\frac{1}{2}$ inches (89 mm) across, while the present example is $2\frac{1}{2}$ inches (63 mm). The handles are a very good imitation of the early eighteenth-century design, but they are marginally too thick and the pommels are secured with machine-made brass nuts. On looking at a modern lock from the back, all one can see is a brass plate, inside which are steel wards which mate with the shape of the key. On eighteenth-century locks, however, the fixing of the steel wards into the brass plate can be seen from the outside. They are not visible on this example (Plate 29).

The use of burr ash as a timber in this piece was an intelligent variation of the burr walnut theme, and certainly lends an air of authenticity, but it is quite definitely a reproduction, and on even closer examination pretends to be nothing else.

Much attractive oak furniture was made after around 1700, but mostly in country areas where craftsmen had not so much ability to make finely crafted joints and were usually without an appreciation of the finer points of design. London cabinet-makers at this time, even by the 1680s, were concentrating their attentions on walnut, which could easily be cut into veneers. Oak furniture was more crudely made and is therefore considered of second-rate manufacture; for this reason oak collectors tend to dismiss anything after about 1700. The sideboard illustrated in Plate 71 may, however, be considered worthy of attention, although it was made as late as 1720. Its size and proportions are delightful, measuring 56 inches (1420 mm) long, 18 inches (460 mm) deep and 30 inches (760 mm) high. It is made entirely of good, dark honey-coloured oak, and where it has not been polished it shades to much darker tones, most noticeable round the ogee (or onion) arches.

The three drawers are thickly lined in oak, with rounded top edges to the linings and with broad, but crude, dovetails. These suggest a date of about 1720, as do the handles which are quite

original (Plate 25c) – this categorical statement is based on the fact that there are no indications in the woodwork that other handles have ever been present. The vase baluster turnings of the legs could be mistaken for a seventeenth-century design, and the mouldings on the drawer edges, beneath the top and round the platform base would be reason to strengthen this argument. The rails and muntins are held by single pegs, and the top is also pegged. However, there is no doubt at all that the drawers are original to its construction and the piece must be dated to its latest feature. The ogee arches between the column supports were also much in vogue in the 1720s and, although it was common to shape the frieze of a sideboard in the seventeenth century, this particular design is eighteenth century. Such pieces were also made with upper sections of shelves, when they were called dressers, and were intended for the display of pewter and pottery. One should look for marks where this section might have been fitted.

   Comparison between this piece and the sideboard illustrated in Plate 88 shows how little the design of such objects changed in country areas. One can easily imagine this piece with

71 Small oak sideboard, country-made c. 1720.

cupboards below the drawers instead of turned legs and a platform shelf. By the same token one can imagine the sideboard in Plate 88 as standing on legs and a platform base instead of the cupboards. It is interesting that one is able to date these pieces by constructional detail.

The walnut chair illustrated in Plate 72 dates from about 1715-20. The back 'moves' in every conceivable direction to combine aesthetic line with anatomical proportions (Plates 37, 38 and 39). The re-entrant corners are a typical decoration of the period, but the scrolls add a touch of individuality and are repeated on the shoe. The splat is a development of the

72 Walnut side chair, c. 1715–20.

inverted vase, and the front surface, which forms the most important piece of show-wood in the chair, is veneered – a feature found only on the finest examples. The seat rails are quite plain and straightforward and it is interesting to note that pegs have been omitted, indicating the craftsman's confidence that he could break away from former techniques and place his trust in the new glues and the quality of his mortise and tenon joints.

The front seat rail is shaped on its lower edge to complement the curves of the back and the rear seat rail is numbered VIII. Quite correctly, this has been done with a chisel, and each stoke is approximately $\frac{5}{8}$ inch (15.8 mm) long. Chairs were always numbered in this fashion, and should one find numbers or joints numbered with Arabic numerals, then either they were made at a later date, or the chair has been taken apart and reassembled. The front legs are cabriole and the knees are carved with a curious stylised shell, from which hangs a flower and three spots. The feet are in the form of a shoe, and are commonly known as Manx feet. It should be noticed that carving on the knee of a cabriole should always stand proud of the general shape. Plain cabriole legs have been often decorated since they were made, and to do this the carver has to cut into an existing shape. When assessing the originality or otherwise of such a leg, it is important to check that it does stand out from the general shape of the leg or foot.

The centre stretcher here has a ribbed motif, echoing the shell carving on the knee. The rear legs move and swell to accept the stretchers, which must therefore have been an

73 The numbering on the rear seat rail of the chair in Plate 72. Each stroke of the roman numerals is always made by a single blow of a chisel struck by a mallet.

74 Detail of a front leg of the chair in Plate 72. Note the fluency of the carving which stands proud of the surrounding leg shape.

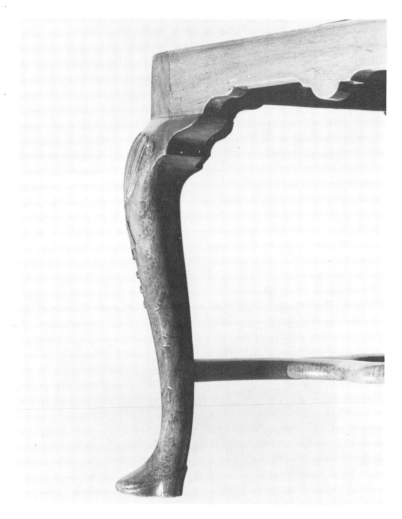

integral part of the design. In order to accommodate the upholstered drop-in or trap seat, the seat rails are rebated.

Many dealers refer to such chairs as spoonbacks, and because they are generally in walnut they are said to be Queen Anne; however, modern thinking would give more credence to a George I label. They pre-date the broader backed variety, with the top rail becoming lower and the seat rails tending to be bell shaped. A former head of department at the Victoria and Albert Museum once said that he had never seen a finer example than this chair. However, it can be argued that the comparable lacquer chairs were more highly valued when originally made, and it is not unknown for a chair of this date or later to be covered with gesso and gilded. Such a chair would be regarded as being of the highest importance, as would a chair decorated in lacquer, because of the frail nature of the decoration.

75 Walnut chair of *c.* 1720, of rustic proportions and with arms added some eighty years later.

In the text accompanying Plates 72 and 77, two chairs with close similarities have already been described. The chair illustrated here in Plate 75 is of the same type, often called Queen Anne, as can be seen from the general outline of the back, the cabriole legs and the stretchers. This example, however, has neither the carved decoration, the veneered splat or the carved legs; it is constructed in solid walnut and the various members are pegged together. It is also lacking the anatomical outline of the others, and the height and width are much less generous.

The arms are perhaps the most interesting features of this chair. Arms of this design were quite unknown in 1720 when this chair was originally made, but the same type are often seen in chairs manufactured in 1800-10. If the reader can imagine the arms removed, the whole chair assumes a more realistic proportion, but even then the back is a good deal smaller than that of the chair in Plate 72. Originally this chair had a drop-in seat, but it has been replaced by a solid seat of oak, and given a loose squab cushion to make this comfortable.

The front legs also look very unfinished at their upper end, for a cabriole leg should have 'ears' to give it a finished appearance. These are fixed separately, as the cabinet-maker would require a piece of wood 6 inches (152 mm) square at least to make the whole cabriole from one piece. During the life of this chair the glue securing the ears to the leg has perished and the ears have been lost. Presumably the cabinet-maker realised that glue was not good enough for major joints and relied on pegs to keep the rest of the chair together. From the surface and polish where the ears should be, it is clear that they parted company a very considerable time ago. Nonetheless, the cabriole legs swell very delightfully to receive the 'H'-shaped stretcher. Notice how the turned section of the stretcher fits into the turned front leg, but the square back leg receives a square section of stretcher.

No part of this chair is less than 175 years old and therefore, in a strict sense, it must certainly be called antique. Whether, because it has been altered and added to during its life, it can be called 'genuine' is another matter. Certainly there is nothing fake or in any way deceiving about it, and undoubtedly the chair has a very considerable charm. It is very typical of a large number of pieces of furniture on the market today.

Bedroom furniture usually includes a chest of drawers as well as cupboards. If one chest is not enough, there are two alternatives – either to have a second chest, or to increase the height of the first chest to such an extent that it becomes virtually one chest upon another. In America such pieces are still called 'chest on chests', but in Britain they are called tallboys. They made their debut at the turn of the eighteenth century, and soon developed into the sophistication of the example illustrated in Plate 76.

As is common, the upper section has three small drawers at the top. Above them is a complicated moulding of general concave outline. The arrangement of drawers is much as one would expect in a chest of drawers, a neat graduation, increasing towards the bottom. The present example is of finely figured walnut, inlaid some $\frac{1}{2}$ inch (12.7 mm) in from each edge with the most delicate arrangement of boxwood and ebony in a chequered design. This is an elegant variation on the more usual herringbone or feather banding theme. The figure of the timber, moreover, is of such interest that it continues right to the edge of the drawer rather than being bordered with a cross-banding, which is more common.

The drawers are fitted with pierced plate handles which retain their original gilding, and escutcheons to match. It will be noted that the handles of the three short drawers on the top incorporate the escutcheon, as do the short drawers below; this is quite normal. The drawers are outlined in cock beading and are lined with finest quarter-cut wainscot oak, $\frac{1}{4}$ inch (6 mm) thick with rounded top edges. The grain of the drawer bottom runs from back to front and the drawers are flanked by a fluted pilaster column on the canted angles. The lower section is marginally wider than the top and the difference is made good on the waist with a cross grained moulding.

The lower section is decorated in much the same way as the upper, but the top drawer opens and hinges downwards to reveal a shaped secretaire interior, fitted with drawers, pigeon holes and a cupboard in much the same way as a bureau. As one would expect of such a very fine article, the small interior drawers are also lined in walnut and the linings are less than an $\frac{1}{8}$ inch (3 mm) thick. The quality of the dovetails is superb, even though they are rather widely spaced. The cupboard and drawers are inlaid like the larger drawers and the cupboard door, with its mirror, is flanked by a pair of simulated pilasters of inlaid boxwood.

The lower section is flanked by a slightly wider pair of pilasters which terminate with an ogee mould at their base, but perhaps one of the most desirable features of this piece is the shape of the bottom drawer and of the bottom moulding to accommodate it. It has been cut at its centre with a niche and

76 Unusually finely crafted walnut tallboy, incorporating a secretaire drawer and the sun-burst motif, *c.* 1735.

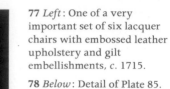

77 *Left*: One of a very important set of six lacquer chairs with embossed leather upholstery and gilt embellishments, *c.* 1715.

78 *Below*: Detail of Plate 85. Note the general colour and variety of grain of the walnut. Pieces of veneer can easily become separated during the gluing of the burr figures to the ground wood, and it was therefore sometimes necessary to patch. Two such patches are visible in the top drawer front.

79 *Opposite*: A very fine mahogany breakfront bookcase, *c.* 1760 owing much to the designs of Thomas Chippendale, and probably made by his firm.

inlaid in boxwood and ebony to simulate a sunburst. This motif is repeated on the floor of the secretaire drawer and is one of the most highly prized motifs on walnut furniture. The base-mould, like all the others, is of cross-grain timber, and the whole piece sits on ogee bracket feet of shaped outline.

The ends of the tallboy are well-figured walnut of halved veneers and are finished on both the back and front with cross-banding. More usually such furniture was finished in very plain timber or even in pine. It would be most unusual, however, having seen the quality of the inlays, the sunburst, the inclusion of the secretaire drawer, the ogee bracket feet and the cross grained mouldings to find an end of any less quality. In other words, the consistency of quality is total. It is when the quality varies within a piece that one's suspicions as to its authenticity are aroused.

Plate 81 shows a George II oak lowboy, or three-drawer side-table of about 1730. The top comprises three planks of quarter-cut oak, exhibiting 'silver fleck' or medullary rays. A cross-banding of walnut some $\frac{3}{4}$ inch (19 mm) wide has been let into the edge, which has been moulded. It will be noticed that the top is thinner than on earlier furniture and the moulding exaggerates this effect. The apron, or frieze, is shaped at the

81 Oak three-drawer side table, or lowboy, *c.* 1730, of good design but less desirable than its walnut counterpart.

sides with a simple ogee arch (note the similarity with the arches on the oak sideboard in Plate 71), and in the front is fretted around a knee-hole and accommodates three short drawers.

When opened, the drawers reveal thin pine linings with coarse dovetails (Plate 25d); the tops of the linings are round, which is a typical feature of the period. Examination inside shows no signs of this piece ever having had another set of handles: indeed the present set look as if they have never been moved. The brass nuts which hold the pommels of the handles have not been marked by spanners or pliers, and there are no tell-tale scratches on the wood. The drawer fronts are decorated in the same way as the top with cross-banding of walnut on an oak ground, and the cross-banding is mitred at the corners. Outside the banding is a simple quarter-round or ovolo moulding which is flush with the sides of the drawers. The brassplate handles are typical of their period and it will be noticed that they are not quite central, especially in the case of the centre drawer.

This lowboy shows good design and aspects such as the cross-banding indicate that the cabinet-maker was highly skilled, although not necessarily London based. Were the piece of the finest quality it would have been veneered with walnut on all the main surfaces and outlined in herringbone or feather banding as well as cross-banding. The cabriole legs, which end in simple pad feet, would have been solid walnut and the drawer linings, while of similar thickness, would have been wainscot oak, probably with better dovetails (Plate 25e).

Some cross-banding is missing from the left-hand drawer and from the top. However, there is no visible sign of restoration. When the top is examined with a powerful magnifying glass, numerous tiny, and some slightly larger, scratches appear, but not a single one stops at the junction of the oak and the cross-banding. There is therefore no reason for doubting the authenticity of the banding.

In the finest houses, reception rooms were arranged along the exterior walls of the house, with tall windows divided by masonry divisions called piers. These rooms were for formal entertainment, suitable to the social stature of the owners of the house, and it was almost obligatory to furnish them in the prevailing fashion – namely a table at each pier with a looking glass above it. A formal arrangement of seat furniture would have been set about the periphery of such a room and these chairs would be moved as the occasion demanded. Of course,

82 One of a pair of console tables of carved and gilded wood, possibly designed by William Kent, *c.* 1740.

such furniture was rare in the first place, as only the grandest houses were so equipped.

The tables were generally large, with mirrors of corresponding proportions above them, and it is therefore a delight to see such a small pier table as that in Plates 82 and 83. The top is rectangular, with double re-entrant corners, and a moulding all round the edge. The whole table is gilded; the top is decorated in gesso with a symmetrical pattern of foliage and acorns, scrolls and strapwork, scallop shells and garya husks, all in low relief against a hatched background. The frieze is below a carved acanthus moulding and is decorated with Vitruvian scrolls, with foliage at the corners and a scallop shell in the centre. The main support is a vigorously modelled eagle carved in the round and perched on a plinth, carved in sympathy with the top with acanthus foliage, and on a base moulding of unequal guilloche, with flowerhead paterae within the circles.

The table dates from about 1740 and is the product of a specialist maker. With further research it might be feasible to attribute this to the workshops of Gumley, Grendey or Moore. Even now, fine houses often retain records of such purchases, including the maker of the original furniture. These archives

provide a fascinating source of reference for academics studying furniture, as it is sometimes possible to ascribe a maker to a piece of furniture about which very little had previously been known. In the same room as the present example (which is one of a pair), there is another pair with several characteristics in common with it. It is known that William Kent worked in the house and a design attribution to him may be plausible.

The card table shown in Plate 84 dates from about 1745, and exhibits some of the best and worst features of antique furniture. Whether its merits outweigh its shortcomings is a matter of where one draws the line and this I will leave the reader to decide. The rectangular top is of plain San Domingo mahogany and opens to reveal a baize-lined interior. Each corner projects from the rectangular outline, and is recessed to accommodate a mahogany square on which a candlestick would stand to illuminate the game. In many tables of similar design, a shallow bowl-shaped depression, about 3 inches (76 mm) deep and 2 inches (51 mm) wide, would be adjacent to

83 Detail of the top of the console in Plate 82. This elaborate decoration rendered the table quite useless for any purpose other than decoration.

120

84 A mahogany card table with carved decoration to the frieze and cabriole legs finishing in claw and ball feet. It dates from about 1745 and details of its construction are shown in Plate 33.

each candlestick square, to accommodate counters or chips. Normally one either finds both candlestick stands and counter wells, or else neither, and it is rare to find the one without the other.

The apron is of cross-grained timber and accommodates perhaps the most desirable feature of the table, the concertina action (Plate 33). This allows the piece, when opened, to have a leg at each corner and to appear symmetrical. Below the frieze is a bold moulding of gadrooning (Plate 40) with a small carved motif in the middle. The cabriole legs are well drawn from a large piece of timber, and decorated at the head with carved acanthus leaves spreading from a concave cabochon. It is particularly noteworthy that the decoration is hipped, that is it extends above the cabriole leg and on to the apron. This is a most unusual feature, reserved for finest quality English furniture of this period. The ears are carved with a flame motif spreading from the inside of a 'C' scroll. The feet are of the claw and ball variety, and are vigorously carved, but perhaps one might have liked the ball to be deeper and for more talon to be visible on the end of the claw. Nonetheless there is no meanness in the design, and it is evidently original, for there is no way such a foot could be carved from the end of a pad foot.

Now for the disadvantage! Close examination will reveal that this card table has been restored. The back legs, while original, are joined by a back rail which has been replaced quite recently. Worse still, this rail has an applied gadrooned moulding, and that too has been replaced. A comparison of the crispness of carving and of the surface between these parts and the rail at the front of the piece, will be instructive. Moreover, there is a join some $1\frac{3}{4}$ inches (44 mm) from the back of the top, and this also is a replacement. The top of such card tables is always from one piece of wood and a join immediately arouses suspicion. In other words the piece has been the subject of considerable abuse at some time during its life. The back had obviously become distressed to such a condition that the restorer felt unable to repair the old wood and had to replace it with another piece of timber. The colour and surface are almost what one would expect, as a good old surface has been used, but there are no lines of dirt in the carving on the cabriole legs, or at the junction between the flat surfaces and the carving. The restorer apparently decided to strip the whole piece of furniture and to re-polish it at the same time.

Since the concertina action has not been entirely replaced, we can conclude that the table was originally made in this manner, and looked exactly as it does now. The restoration is not in the nature of an 'improvement', but the fastidious collector may not entertain the idea of acquiring such a piece. Commercially it is worth perhaps half or even less than the same article which has survived intact and unrestored. However, many people who wish to furnish their houses with good-looking furniture are unable to afford the very high prices that such items fetch when they are in an ideal condition. The present example has the same value as an unrestored piece without any carving, with pad feet, and with a plain baize-lined interior, the top supported on a gate-leg action rather than a concertina. It is for the reader to decide which is the better bargain.

In Chapter 2 it was explained that the supply of walnut had dwindled considerably by the 1720s and the vast proportion of fine cabinet-making was then executed in mahogany. The love of walnut, however, did not diminish, and cabinet-makers of quality retained stocks of their finest walnut timbers. The knee-hole desk illustrated in Plate 85 is evidence of this, for it dates from about 1745-50. The top, curiously, is of halved

85 Walnut knee-hole desk. These were made from about 1690, and the handles, bracket feet and mouldings on this example suggest a date of about 1745.

veneers – one might have expected them to be quartered – and is of relatively plain grain. The cross-banding is wide, at nearly an inch (25 mm), but the feather banding is quite narrow, less than $\frac{1}{4}$ inch (6 mm).

The chest of drawers in Plate 69 had a quarter round moulding to the top, and this design was superseded by the cross-banded edge with a small quarter round moulding above it. Usually such a moulding had re-entrant corners (page 168). This in turn gave way to the thumb moulded edge, first done in cross-grained timber and later made long-grain. The present example is a cross-grain thumb moulding veneered on to a triangular section of pine.

The drawers are arranged in a typical layout for a knee-hole desk, three on either side of a recessed cupboard, itself below a flush 'secret' drawer at the top of the knee-hole. The drawers are veneered in the finest burr walnut, outlined with feather banding and cross-banded in a straight grain timber. They are edged with a cock bead of solid walnut and are even veneered on walnut – a truly unusual feature. The drawer linings are in the finest wainscot oak, and the dovetails are of very good quality, ending in a point. The drawer bottoms are rebated into the linings with the grain running from side to side, and the drawer moves on a pair of runners glued to the bottoms. The locks are still made of iron and are almost square.

The handles are perhaps the most obvious dating feature of this piece: they quite clearly show a Rococo influence, although this is not manifest in the backplate. The escutcheons are finely cast in the Rococo style. The carcase is cross-banded throughout in straight grain walnut, but the mouldings are in cross-grain timber. Original, but somewhat archaic, are the 'H' hinges on the knee-hole cupboard, which encloses one shelf. Occasionally, but not on this example, knee-hole cupboards slide forward like a drawer so that the whole cupboard ends up flush with the drawer fronts. If the reader notices wear on the base moulding and on the sides of a knee-hole this would indicate that the cupboard does slide forward. The bracket feet are typical and are held in position with glued blocks.

Had this example been in mahogany, which it could well have been, a date of 1770 might seem more likely. However, the plain back plates to the handles, the use of cross-grained mouldings, and the use of walnut for the whole piece put the date we have given beyond question.

William Kent and Robert Adam drew on classical forms for their inspiration, but their products are never considered reproductions. No doubt occasional copies were made to make up a pair even in the eighteenth century, but the first reproductions as such were made in the nineteenth century. It has been mentioned that in the 1830s the Gothic taste was revived, and that not long after that the elaborate decoration of the Rococo was copied. The chair illustrated in Plate 86 is quite typical of the era, being manufactured around 1840-60. The interlaced, pierced and inverted vase-shaped splat does not appear in Thomas Chippendale's *Director*, written some eighty years previously, but it might easily have done so. The top rail is of the serpentine form typical of Chippendale's designs, and is outlined in 'C' scrolls and terminates in a little acanthus foliage. The stiles are well moulded and shaped, as is the back. The stuff-over seats upholstered in leather are bordered with two rows of brass studs. The legs are not only moulded, but are supported at the ears with carved brackets and sit on diminutive plinths conforming in outline to the mouldings.

How, then, is one to distinguish between a genuine chair and this example? The design is nearly perfect. The first clue lies in the brilliant polish, which is not an accumulation of waxes, but varnish. This appears to be quite original. In the Chippendale period, timber of a uniform quality was freely available, but in

86 Mahogany dining chair (one of a set of eight) of Chippendale style. The lack of stretchers and the lack of chamfering of the back of the splat are easy contrasts to the two period chairs in Plate 3.

the nineteenth century this was no longer the case, and there are members in the present example, noticeably the shoe, where stains had to be applied to match one piece of timber with another. This would not be found on an original. Chippendale-designed chairs have stretchers unless they have cabriole legs. They always have stretchers uniting the front and back legs in an 'H' arrangement, with an additional stretcher uniting the rear legs. The stretchers are not present on this example, nor are there signs where stretchers have once been tenoned into the legs and since removed.

The upholstery is original to the chair, but in eighteenth-century examples the brass studs would have been closer spaced. Still more is revealed when the chair is inverted. The

seat rails, quite correctly, are made of beech, but they are covered with stain to simulate age. One would expect $\frac{1}{2}$ inch (12.7 mm) square braces at the front and side rails as in Plate 35, but triangular blocks take their place. The seat rails are marginally thicker than in eighteenth-century chairs, and where the brackets have shrunk and the glue has come away, the original colour of the timber can be seen beneath. That the seat rails are stained is clear not only from the evidence above, but also at the places where hands have rubbed the sides of the rails – they show paler where the stain has been removed, instead of darker where dirt would would have accumulated over many years.

The present example is also stamped with a letter and a four-figure number, a practice very common in the nineteenth century, indicating the serial number of the design from the workshop from which it came. Finally there are small brackets tying the seat rails to the back legs. This, and the proportion of the back seat rail, is again incompatible with construction of eighteenth-century furniture.

On some occasions one is confronted with an object which defies any attempt to establish an obvious date. The oak sideboard illustrated in Plate 88 is a good example of this. It is exactly what it appears to be, namely three drawers below a moulded top and beneath that a pair of cupboards flanking a dummy cupboard. The whole piece has a very good colour and patina, and is supported on diminutive and simple bracket feet. It may well be thought that this sideboard was the lower half of a dresser, but an upper section would have left marks of its fixing, and no such marks exist. One may therefore take it that the piece is an entity.

There are several points worthy of note. The top is cleated, that is it has a strip of wood running along each end with the grain in the opposite direction to the main top planks. It is considered good cabinet-making to edge with long grain timber and this is one method of doing so. On the finest quality pieces, the cleat is mitred at its corners as in the table in Plate 66, but here the easy way out has been taken and the cleat runs to the edge. The moulding round the top gives the first indication that this piece of oak is not seventeenth century; it is ovolo with a further cavetto moulding applied beneath the top. This is repeated on the base moulding. The main carcase is, as one would expect, made with stiles, rails and muntins. What is noticeable, however, is that not all the rails are pegged, although of course they are mortised and tenoned. This also indicates that the piece is later than seventeenth century.

The drawers do not retain their original handles and, although the ones fitted are late seventeenth century, close examination will reveal holes where previous sets of handles have existed. Looking behind the drawer front the observer

88 Oak sideboard dating from the second half of the eighteenth century. The handles pre-date it by some eighty years.

can see three sets of handle holes, and one set is obviously original as the area cut away to accommodate the handle is the same colour as the surrounding wood. Marks where this hole has been can still be traced on the front of the drawer, as can the outline of the handle which went through it. The drawer linings are quite thick, indicating that the piece was made in the provinces, but the dovetails are quite fine which would indicate a later date.

The oval escutcheon plates on the drawers would appear to be original, and are surrounded by a very pleasant patination. The cupboards and dummies are fielded panels. This type of decoration was popular in a shaped form from about 1710-20, after which it became square or rectangular as in the present example, and remained fashionable until about 1780. In the Channel Islands fielded panels continued to be made in mahogany pieces until the end of the century. Still we have not solved the problem of date. Clearly, although the piece is made of oak, it cannot be seventeenth century, and the fielded panels indicate a date after 1720. The case is arguable, but owing to the quality of the dovetails, the type of moulding on the top, and the likely form of handle before the present ones, one suspects that this piece may date from about 1770 and that it was probably made somewhere far away from the centres of fashionable production, perhaps in Somerset or Devonshire. What is strongly borne out by this piece is that one cannot date a piece earlier than its latest original constituent part.

A great deal of eighteenth-century furniture is thought to be important because of its monumental proportions, its gilded enrichments, or the exotic timbers used in its manufacture, but the collector of English furniture does not necessarily regard these features as the sole criteria of desirability. The little cabinet in Plate 89 measures only $18\frac{3}{8}$ inches (467 mm) high, $13\frac{1}{2}$ inches (343 mm) wide, and $7\frac{1}{4}$ inches (184 mm) deep and yet embodies all the fine points that a collector could wish for. To start with, it is rare. It seems that the only diminutive hanging wall cupboards to be found are encountered in the large houses of the wealthy. They were presumably intended to house a pair of works of art of great value and obviously such objects would not be found in a humble household.

In the second place the cupboard illustrated here is quite untouched by a restorer; the wood has never been stripped, cleaned and re-polished and yet there is no open grain. The surface has a deep even and mellow shine. One would hardly expect to see signs of wear on an article such as this, and in fact

89 Small hanging wall cabinet in San Domingo mahogany displaying the influence of the Gothic revival, *c.* 1770.

the mouldings and all the edges are crisp. The mouldings are well designed and somewhat uncommon, and fine quality San Domingo timber has been used in the making throughout.

A particularly interesting point to the collector is the very obvious Gothic influence. One of the great arbiters of taste during the mid-eighteenth century was Horace Walpole, whose house at Strawberry Hill near Twickenham sparked off the first of the Gothic revivals. It had a marked effect upon designers at the time and this cabinet, while being of very ordinary eighteenth-century design in many respects, has the Gothic ogee arch, clearly stamping the Strawberry Hill influence. The ogee has two distinct advantages in being both attractive to look at and useful for the display of small objects.

Thus it is that a rather small, unpretentious cabinet can have a large number of attributes that the collector wants – rarity, academic interest, surface, quality, colour, aesthetic appeal and small size, an advantage that makes its use compatible with living in modern houses.

Early on in the design of bookcases it was realised that a box-like form was aesthetically uninteresting. A solution to this problem was soon found by simply dividing the piece into sections and recessing either end in relation to the centre. This construction also had the advantage of being easily dismantled for transportation, and was called a breakfront bookcase.

The breakfront bookcase illustrated in Plate 79 is a superbly proportioned example, strongly influenced by the designs of Thomas Chippendale. The architectural cornice, with its broken triangular pediment, is delicately moulded with ogee and concave moulds above a dentil section. The broken pediment is filled with diaper lattice work and the whole cornice is closely modelled on Chippendale's 'Chinese frets'. The bookcase section has three doors enclosing adjustable shelves. The central cupboard has a thirteen panel glazed door with astragal mouldings framing the glazing, flanked by delicately fretted pilasters each with an elongated, pierced carved scroll of delightful execution. The side cupboards are not glazed, but instead are fronted with brass wire, producing a honeycomb pattern.

Below the bookcase section is a waist mould above a band of Greek key blind fret, which hides the presence of three drawers (perhaps you can see the key holes). Below this again are three cupboard doors with the centre conforming to the cupboard above, being flanked with a pair of blind frets. The cupboard door itself is a shaped, fielded panel with well-chosen quarter veneers and cross-banded on the bevel. The corners set into the fielded panels are outlined with another 'Chinese fret', and this cupboard is flanked in turn by a pair of similar cupboards decorated in the same fashion. The whole is on a plinth of conforming outline moulded on its upper edge.

Perhaps this piece has everything that a connoisseur of fine furniture could wish for: small size, elegant proportions, (they are anything up to 20 feet (6 m) long – this one is less than 6 feet (2 m), superb craftsmanship, and imaginative use of timbers. The condition is exemplary, with splendid patination and surface – the bookcase has always been well looked-after – yet it still betrays signs of its age: for example, the waist mould is slightly scratched where the door has opened over a piece of grit. There are slight indentations where the occasional foot has marked the plinth. These very minor points in no way detract from its prodigious appeal to the collector.

If the chest of drawers illustrated in Plate 90 were to appear in a catalogue compiled by one of the auction houses, it might well

90 Mahogany chest of drawers of Lancashire origin, with Cuban mahogany matched veneers, and with brass swan neck handles, c. 1770.

be described as follows: 'An early George III mahogany chest of two short and three long graduated drawers, the top well figured and with a moulded edge, the drawers with cock beading and original gilt brass swan-neck handles, resting on a shaped moulding and ogee bracket feet. 45 inches (1143 mm) long, 32 inches (812 mm) high, 22 inches (558 mm) deep. Circa 1770.'

Throughout the eighteenth century a considerable number of chests of drawers were made. The overall configuration remained almost unaltered, but the *minutiae* of construction and points of finishing followed the trends of fashion prevalent at the period in which they were made. Early eighteenth-century chests, for example, had half round mouldings on the carcase (Plates 61 and 69), while mid-eighteenth-century ones had cock beading on the drawer edge (Plates 76, 85). Early bun feet gave way to later bracket feet, and so on. With rare exceptions chests of drawers came in three shapes: the straight, the bow front and the serpentine front (in the same order of difficulty to make and held today in a corresponding degree of

91 *Far left*: The canted corner of a serpentine chest of drawers inlaid with a satyr mask and a trail of fruit and flowers.

92 *Left*: Canted corner of a tallboy and with applied carving. The fruit and flowers in this instance are carved.

93 *Opposite*: Mahogany inlaid corner cabinet. Oval panels and stringing used in this manner often cause such a piece to be called 'Sheraton'. In fact it pre-dates his work and owes little to his design, *c.* 1780.

esteem). While the crudest serpentines have straight sides, better ones have canted corners, and it is this feature that lends itself to still further improvement and embellishment. The canting may be fluted or, even better, fluted and reeded like the leg of the Pembroke table (Plate 104) and the corner of the tallboy (Plate 76), and later examples are sometimes inlaid with boxwood to simulate fluting; but the most desirable are those carved or inlaid with foliage, fruit, flowers or other Rococo motifs.

Sometimes the two short drawers were substituted by one long one, and sometimes above that were slides, either for writing or (supposedly) for brushing clothes on. Another variation was the inclusion of fitments in the top drawer to provide the requisites of writing or dressing (considered by some collectors to be a bonus). In such cases the top drawer can be fitted with a ratchetting mirror, powder boxes, compartments and so on, whereas the writing drawer will be fitted with a writing or reading slide and stationery divisions, ink wells and pen trays.

The desirability of chests of drawers depends on several factors. First is the proportion; chests of drawers not more than 32 inches (812 mm) high are considered suitable for reception rooms, whereas if they are higher than this they are thought to be made for bedrooms. The most valuable chests of drawers are very narrow, say 24 inches (609 mm) to 32 inches (812 mm) wide; but anything on the upper limit or larger tends to make a chest less wanted because these too are assumed to be for

Straight

bow

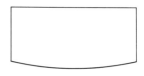

serpentine shapes

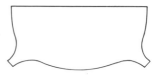

133

94 *Below*: Rosewood and
satinwood secretaire cabinet
with bookshelf
superstructure. The
quartered veneers are of
rosewood and the oval panels
West Indian satinwood.
c. 1790.

95 *Opposite*: Bureau bookcase
of typical proportions, made
in Jersey *c.* 1800.

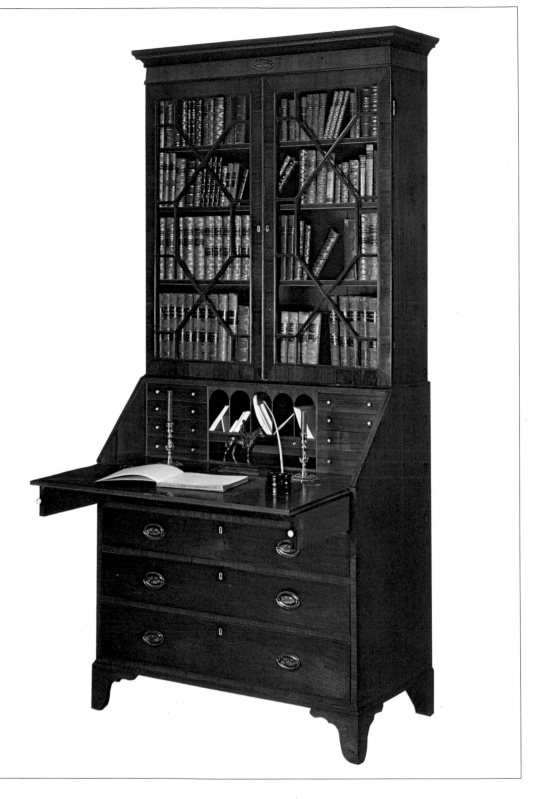

96 *Left*: Mahogany bracket clock by Walter Mitchelson with enamelled dials and brass mounts, *c*. 1795.

97 *Below*: An important Regency coromandel wood centre table supported on gilt wood griffins, *c*. 1815.

bedrooms. However, if the width exceeds 44 inches (1117 mm) and the piece is lower than 34 inches (864 mm) it will suddenly fit into another category and be called a commode. This is merely an adaptation of the French word and has nothing to do with the cupboard containing a chamber pot, called by the same name.

The example illustrated dates from around 1770, and has unusually wide proportions for a straight-front chest of drawers. The drawer linings are of oak and the handles retain their original gilding. The mouldings are good and crisp and, apart from the shrinkage in the sides, it is in an unusually good and unrestored condition. The drawer fronts are veneered with well chosen, matched veneers, as is the top. This is a desirable item as straight fronted chests of drawers go, but had it been 6 inches (152 mm) taller and broader it would be considerably less valuable, worth perhaps 80 per cent less.

The chest of drawers illustrated in Plate 98 is an example of the quaint and amusing in the study of English furniture. It has

98 A quaint mahogany chest of drawers, which, viewed from the top, is rhomboid in shape, c. 1770.

some similarities with the chest illustrated in Plate 90: the handles and mouldings are almost identical, and it was made at much the same date. Where the other is classically conventional in its arrangement of drawers and proportions, however, the present example shows the height of individuality. The whole chest is rhomboidal in shape. The top is oak and has a hinged compartment opening only with a key. It is calibrated in inches at its left-hand end – whether this feature is original is impossible to say, but it has certainly been there for most of the chest's life. The compartment revealed when the lid is opened is only 2 inches (51 mm) deep, but it slopes, being deeper at the back than at the front.

The carcase is of pine on the right hand side, and of mahogany on the left, while the drawer fronts are well-figured Cuban mahogany lined in pine and with fairly coarse dovetails. The cock beading is of the simulated scratched type, being merely an incision in the drawer front. To conform with the shape of the piece the drawers have to slide out and up, because of the wedge-shape of the top compartment. The moulding above the shaped bracket feet is typical of the 1770s as is the half round

99 Detail of the top left hand edge of the chest. Note the calibrations, the scratch beading and the detail of the handles. Such precision is not found in reproduction handles.

moulding that edges the top. Had this piece been of fine London production it would have had four drawers instead of three, and perhaps a brushing slide above them. However, it has an enormous charm, with a degree of sophistication which is quite unexpected, and is just the sort of thing many people today seek for their small flats and houses. Its somewhat absurd configuration and mixture of sophistication with rustic crudeness give it a unique appeal.

In the eighteenth century, just as today, one could either buy furniture from stock, or cabinet-makers would construct an object to a client's specific requirements. This chest of drawers obviously falls into the latter category, while the chest in Plate 90 may well have been in the former. It was mentioned earlier that consistency of quality should be sought, but a very fine article is occasionally made with pine sides. These are usually called fitments, and were made for alcoves or recesses, or other places where the owner knew that the pine would not be seen. When removed from its original position, such a piece is difficult to sell, and commercially minded restorers sometimes veneered the sides to enhance the value.

The commode is an important piece of furniture. It was an object of display in a state apartment or grand room, and although it will accommodate goods, it is perfectly apparent that this is not its prime function. For example the object illustrated in Plate 80 only has three drawers in its centre section as it was not necessary to store a great many objects in reception rooms; they were rooms of entertainment and display and were furnished only so as to give a lived-in appearance. With the exception of chairs and card tables etc. furniture did not have a functional role and was intended primarily to complement the architectural design of the room. It is not surprising, therefore, that commodes should be grand in proportions and concept.

The example illustrated here has a most unusual semi-eliptical top. On the edge of the top is a broad cross-banding consisting of nine rows, the principal one being 2 inches (51 mm) wide and of purple-heart inlaid with boxwood with repeating foliage and honeysuckle, referred to in its stylised form as anthemions. This broad band is outlined with boxwood and ebony and repeated again. The main ground of the top is satinwood inlaid with circular paterae, or fan medallions, of shaded boxwood. In the intervening space is a band of draped garrya husks falling in lobes and secured on its apexes with knots of ribbon. From each knot is suspended an oval medallion with a portrait of inlaid wood. At the centre is a large fan outlined with a chevron banding and centred by a ,curious foliate motif. The edge of the top is inlaid with a running stylised leaf motif. The frieze is of purpleheart inlaid with a most unusual band of motifs of heart-shaped stringing enclosing an anthemoin and tied to the next heart with a circle. The frieze contains one drawer fitted with brass knob handles retaining their original gilding and impressed with a patera. The carcase encloses a single cupboard and is formed from three panels of West,Indian satinwood outlined with broad bands of boxwood and ebony. Each panel is centred by an inlaid plaque copiously decorated and depicting scenes from classical antiquity. The stiles, which support the square tapered legs, are also panel-inlaid, and the legs themselves continue this motif, but are inlaid on their bases with etched boxwood foliage simulating the brass sabots which were in vogue with French furniture. The cupboard door encloses two drawers with mahogany fronts, brass swan neck handles and wainscot oak drawer linings.

The chair illustrated in Plate 100 may well be described as a Hepplewhite chair and dates from about 1780. The shield-shape back has a serpentine top rail delicately moulded at the edges and is inlaid at its apex with a small fan patera. The mouldings continue round the remaining shape of the shield and its supports. The radiating splats are decisively modelled with a wheat ear above a husk, carved stylistically, and they radiate from a half sunflower. The side seat rails are distinctly bowed, enabling the front of the seat to be of generous proportions while the back can be delicate. The front seat rail is similarly bowed to complement the shape. The square tapered legs are fluted below and reeded at the top, and finish in diminutive spade feet. One would expect, on looking underneath the chair, that the seat rails would be beechwood – as in fact they are; they are united by braces.

This chair follows very closely the designs of George Hepplewhite, but not closely enough for one to be able to attribute the design directly to him, although there is certainly a very strong influence. On examining the back of the chair the stiles, the top rail and the outline of the shield are well chamfered in order that they may present a slight profile when viewed from an angle. The same has not been done on the splats which are already thin, though this may have been done had the example been twenty years earlier when the splat would have been cut from a piece of timber twice as thick. The surface

100 Mahogany dining chair with shield-shaped back carved and inlaid, and the stuff over seat supported by square tapered legs, carved and ending in spade feet. The design owes much to George Hepplewhite and dates from about 1780.

and patination leave nothing to be desired on the front, and there is a modicum of darkness where the chair would not have been polished in the ordinary course of household cleaning, but the main surfaces glisten with a warm brown mahogany colour. The back of the back shows several shades of a darker grey where, although the chair has been dusted, it has not been polished. As for wear and tear, there is a slight rounding of the back of the back legs and the front of the front legs, but almost none on the side and certainly none on the inside side edges. The chair has been recently upholstered, but the arrangement of brass studs on the lower edge of the seat rail conforms with contemporary practice, and in fact when the author saw the chair before it was upholstered this arrangement of brass studs was quite clear from marks in the seat rails. It was also considered correct to have a second row of studs at the top of the seat rails and sometimes a geometrical pattern at the head of each leg. The Americans who made similar chairs sometimes arranged their studs to simulate drapery.

During the middle years of the eighteenth century, a number of fine corner cupboards were made as well as some of tolerably good quality. They often had fluted pilaster columns on the sides and usually had panelled doors without glass – called in the trade 'dead', or 'blind', doors. Yet for a reason that has eluded everyone, to my knowledge, corner cupboards made in the latter half of the eighteenth century are usually poor quality. Plate 93 is the exception that proves the rule, as it dates from about 1780 and exhibits the finest craftsmanship of its time.

The swan neck pediment terminates in circular paterae. The scroll on the pediment, too, is composed of a convex moulding with a broad band of sevenfold stringing. The finials when viewed individually look abnormally tall, but viewed from below they assume a much more natural proportion. The upper section of the cabinet comprises one large door. The stiles and rails are very narrow considering the width of the piece, and on both edges are outlined with cross-banding flanked on either side by boxwood and ebony stringing. The glass panels are of rectangular outline, except the top three which are lancet-shaped, and all the glazing bars are faced with a cross-banding similar to the stiles. The glazing bars are correctly made in that they run approximately $\frac{1}{8}$ inch (3 mm) into the stiles and rails when seen from the inside (Plate 30). The door is flanked by a chequered stringing, and the same stringing, cut in half, forms oblong and oval panels in the sides.

The door opens to reveal four shelves, the lowest one being the bottom of the cabinet top. The shelves are elaborately shaped and are made of mahogany, as is the back – a most unusual feature. Running round the perimeter of the inside of the cupboard is a dust stop fillet, approximately $\frac{1}{2}$ inch (12.7 mm) wide, again outlined with chequer stringing and finished attractively with moulding. This latter feature is very rare. The waist mould is approximately the reverse of the cornice and is part of the lower section into which the top sits. Just below this is an arrangement of three drawers, faced with veneers and cross-banding to match those of the door. They are lined with

101 Detail of Plate 93. Note the complexity of the cross banding and stringing lines, the crispness of the mouldings, the evidence of former handles, the construction of the cupboard door (one open and one closed in the photograph), the shaping of the shelf and the fillet inside the cupboard door to prevent dust entering.

Honduras mahogany and the bottoms have grain running from back to front – a usual feature for a piece made at this date. The linings of the flanking drawers taper on their outside edge, to conform with the outline of the cabinet itself.

Although the knob handles are contemporary, they are not original and marks can be seen surrounding them where other handles have been. Below the drawers is a pair of cupboards enclosing one more shaped shelf. The doors, while appearing flat on the outside, reveal a panelled construction when opened. They are veneered with quartered timbers outlined like the drawers and the door above, and centring on a figured oval outlined with further chequered stringing. The base moulding is cavetto and the whole piece stands on shaped bracket feet, but it will be noticed that even the base has a small amount of shaping. The cabinet-maker has selected his timbers most carefully throughout, and has veneered them in such a way that maximum advantage is taken of the fine quality woods he used.

Plate 102 illustrates a mahogany table with two flaps. One flap is supported by a gate (or fly) leg, while the other is shown in the

102 An unassuming but quite genuine mahogany dining table, *c.* 1780-90. The utilitarian and pleasant, if not exciting qualities, contrast with some of the greater productions in the other illustrations.

folded position. The top is composed of three planks with a rule joint between each; the edge is unmoulded and quite unadorned, as is the frieze; and the legs are square, unmoulded, and not even chamfered on the inside edge. The fly leg hinges at a knuckle joint (illustrated on page 55), a method used in a great many card and dining tables of the period. The mahogany is fine quality San Domingo timber, of good grain and colour, simple figure and excellent surface, being quite undisturbed. This table measures 42 inches (1067 mm) by $21\frac{1}{2}$ inches (540 mm), and 63 inches (1600 mm) when extended, and provides seating accommodation for six, eight, or even ten people, depending on the proximity of the diners. There are no visible signs of restoration or repair and with all these features one might be excused for feeling that here was a fine and valuable antique – but here the praise must stop. The piece may not be complete.

Superficially this table seems a fairly typical example of those which originally would have had two additional semi-circular tables, each of identical width and standing on four similar legs, which would have been placed at either end producing a surface some 8 feet (2.4 m) long. Each of these ends might have had an additional flap to extend the table to a total of some 11 feet (3.35 m) long, or one flap might have been omitted. A further alternative is that there might be one or more tables identical to this example fitting between the two half-round (or possibly D-shaped ends), producing a table anything up to 25 feet (7.6 m) long. What might have happened

144

to the remainder of such a dining table can only be a matter for speculation, but perhaps the ends were used as side tables or pier tables and, when this part was sold, the owners did not realise there was more to it than met the eye.

The give-away features that this was part of a larger table would be brass clip holders set in the undersides of each flap, and tongues and grooves in the ends, in order that the table may locate with the other sections. However, these brass fittings do not in fact exist and the undersides of the leaves show no signs whatever of having had any clips or catches. Nor have these been removed by shortening the leaves, for the ends (without tongues or grooves) have an original surface. Here, then, is a Georgian mahogany dining table with simple, unpretentious qualities, surprisingly a complete entity in itself, providing utility, originality, and a very pleasant colour and surface. The timber and square tapered legs date it to about 1780-90.

Another item of furniture beyond the means of most collectors is a set of library steps. Large houses usually contained a library of proportionate size and some books would be perhaps as much as 20 feet (6.1 m) from the ground. It was therefore necessary to equip the library with a means of reaching books on the top shelves. Library steps were developed for this purpose, and they took a great many forms. Sometimes they were disguised as other pieces of furniture, say a table, in which case perhaps a drawer would pull out and pivot about its far end to reveal a set of treads; there was also a variety which, when folded, formed a chair. Examples of these can be seen in National Trust collections and other houses open to the public.

In grander houses, library steps were a piece of furniture in their own right, and the example illustrated here is typical, though not the most grand. It is a straightforward flight of four steps and its configuration can be perfectly well seen from the photograph. The whole is made out of well-chosen San Domingo mahogany, and each tread and other members are cross-banded in tulip wood, with boxwood and ebony stringing on every side. The landing is quarter veneered and similarly cross-banded and centred with an oval satinwood panel, again cross-banded. The landing is bounded by a gallery and hand rail of most delicate and diminutive proportions. More grandiose sets of library steps than the example illustrated here were made with two flights of steps meeting on a landing, and were sometimes fitted with a seat and with a

reading desk so that the user could consult a volume without having to descend. Those illustrated here date from about 1785. This date cannot be accurately deduced from the outline or design of the piece, but is suggested by the decorative detail – note the similarity of the inlaid veneer on the landing with the door fronts of the secretaire illustrated in Plate 94, or the door of the corner cupboard in Plate 93. The same could be said of the arrangement of cross-banding and use of boxwood and ebony stringing.

Library steps like this example serve to indicate both the thoroughness with which a room was furnished and also the consideration that was accorded the original owner – note the quality and degree of care which was lavished on these pieces. One would not expect to find a set of library steps of anything other than fine quality as they were only made for houses with rooms of sufficient height to merit their use. One should therefore regard library steps of bad quality with considerable suspicion.

Many tables made in the eighteenth century have a simple top supported on four legs with a frieze below containing one or more drawers. When such a table has flaps on the long side and a drawer on the short side, it is called a Pembroke table, and Plate 104 illustrates such a piece. A few tables of this variety were made in the 1740s although they are most uncommon, but they were made in abundance from about 1770 onwards. The present example dates from shortly after that time, say 1775, and has a top of serpentine outline. Some people call such tables Butterfly tables, because of the shape of the top. The figure in this one is most unusual, hardly a roe figure, but most reminiscent of the pattern left by the tide-washed sand, or perhaps mackerel sky. The frieze contains one real and one dummy drawer, the former being lined with mahogany approximately $\frac{1}{4}$ inch (6 mm) thick and with the finest of dovetails. The edge of the drawer is cockbeaded, again very finely. The drawer front is veneered with the same timber as on the top and is fitted with a pair of handles formed as three interlocking 'C' scrolls. Tables as well made as this have the dummy looking so like the drawer on the other side that it is difficult, and sometimes even impossible, to tell the difference; even the key hole is simulated. As a result of this the unyielding dummy drawer often has its handles lacking where numerous attempts have been made to pull it out. This table

104 Mahogany Pembroke table, *c.* 1775. The design is restrained and the detail finely carved.

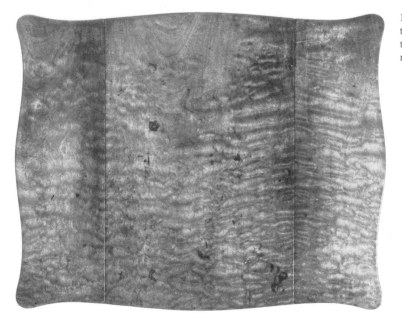

105 The top of the Pembroke table in Plate 104, showing the highly figured Cuban mahogany and gentle outline.

has obviously passed through caring hands as the handles are all original. The legs are square and tapered, but like the chair illustrated in Plate 100 they are reeded and fluted. They terminate in spade feet beneath which are brass box casters retaining their original rollers made of leather, and are headed by finely carved floral oval paterae, crisply executed (Plate 36).

One or two things are worth noting here. Firstly, the author finds the restrained outline of the serpentine top delightful although other people will prefer a bolder outline. Usually the top of such a table is moulded, this example however has an unmoulded cross-banded edge – a delightful conformity to the restraint used elsewhere. The top is of a greyish tan and has never been stripped or repolished, and it has one or two minor stains – the result of fair wear and tear. Again the author considers this is acceptable, but this is a matter of personal opinion. It is the tendency amongst experts now to allow such pieces to remain in their present condition, rather than undertake the wholesale cleaning and repolishing which was carried out by dealers earlier this century.

Plate 94 illustrates a lady's secretaire cabinet, and is the epitome of the refined design that is a feature of the last twenty years of the eighteenth century. The upper section consists of three shelves, the lower one being almost integral with the cabinet below. They are of Brazilian rosewood of a rare restrained figure, the edges are cross-banded and outlined with boxwood stringing as is the gallery over the top shelf. The brass supports are gilded and are headed by urn-shaped finials. It is perhaps worth noting that only the finest quality wood could be used to produce bookshelves of such thin proportions. The lower section has a drawer simulating two drawers, which is decorated on the outside with quarter veneered rosewood with oval panels of satinwood outlined, as is the whole drawer, with tulipwood cross-banding and boxwood stringing. Inside is a simple, neat and symmetrical arrangement of drawers and pigeon-holes veneered with satinwood. The front of the drawer lets down on brass quadrants to reveal a leather writing surface. Beneath the drawer is a pair of cupboards enclosing two mahogany shelves, and the cupboard doors are inlaid in precisely the same way as the drawer front above. Both the doors and the drawer are flanked by panels of satinwood of very stripy-figure outlined with a fine stringing. The whole piece sits on diminutive square tapered legs.

A comparison can be made between this piece and the commode in Plate 80, to which it is the ideal complement and which hardly betters it in importance and quality. The workmanship is superb throughout: the stringing lines are very fine, the matching of the timbers perfect, and the use of wood is most imaginative. It has both elegant proportions and utility. In fact it represents a great many of the attributes that a collector may wish for in forming his collection. Unfortunately pieces like this, in this condition, are most uncommon, and because so many people are looking for them their price is very high, if and when they appear on the market.

By 1780 bureau bookcases had been largely superseded by secretaire bookcases. However, the bureau bookcase illustrated in Plate 95 is an exception to this rule, dating from about 1800, and is worthy of note in many other respects. The upper section has a pair of doors with thirteen-panel glazing. The glazing bars are capped with astragal mouldings, which also run round the whole frame and are repeated on the dust mould (the overlapping moulding between the two doors to stop dust entering the shelves). The doors are cross-banded, with mitring at each corner, and they enclose three shelves made of pine, veneered with purple-heart on the front edge and outlined with boxwood stringing lines. The cornice is cross-banded and inlaid with a bee in an oval medallion in the centre, in much the same way as other pieces of furniture are inlaid with shells or symmetrical paterae. The moulding above is of typical outline for a cornice of this date, and also incorporates a band of inlaid zig-zag white lines on a black background.

If one catches the light against the glass in any of the panes, a very irregular reflection is produced indicating that the glass is hand blown and not of modern manufacture. On examining the inside of the doors, the very narrow glazing bars – less than $\frac{1}{8}$ inch (3 mm) – are found not to be flush with the inside of the doors, a most unusual feature (Plate 30). This means that the glazing bars do not show the rebate in the stiles and rails as one would normally expect.

With all bookcases and china cabinets, the left-hand door is normally secured by two bolts. Each bolt is of gilt brass and rebated into the opening edge of the door. The top bolt is normally longer than the bottom bolt because very often the top of a door is as much as 8 feet (2.4 m) above the ground, whereas the bottom bolt can be reached easily. Once the left-hand door is secured, the right-hand door is made fast against it with a lock. Usually the left-hand door is fitted with an escutcheon or key hole to match the right-hand, but this is for decoration only. The present example has a lock of brass and is rectangular; one can see the steel wards showing through the back of the lock which is rebated into the stile and held with steel screws. The key holes are the skeleton outline type and made of ivory.

The middle section has a fall supported on a pair of lopers and when opened reveals a symmetrical arrangement of pigeon-holes and drawers fitted with their original ivory knobs, as are the lopers. There is a recessed area fitted with baize for writing, and the flap has brass hinges set some 4 inches (102 mm) in from the edge.

Below this arrangement are four long graduated drawers, outlined with cock beads and with ivory skeleton key holes. The handles are oval brass with turned pommels and back plates impressed with agricultural trophies of a wheatsheaf, sickle and vine leaves. These retain their original gilding in a bright state, but the bails, while clean, are lacking their gilding for the most part because they experience the most wear. The carcase is cross-banded between the drawers, which in turn matches the decoration on the edge of the fall. The base moulding, a simple step and a cavetto, repeats the moulding on the top, and the whole piece rests on straightforward bracket feet.

I have already said that this piece is remarkable in several ways. First, the top quite obviously belongs to the bottom, which is not true of a great many bureau bookcases. Here the ivory key holes and the timber can be seen to be identical in both sections, and from the matching mouldings on the base and top it is evident that the bureau always accommodated the upper section. Second, the timber has floored many experts, and until scientific aid is forthcoming one would be foolish to attempt any identification beyond 'rosewood-type'. The cross-banding on the carcase poses a similar problem. Finally, by the small details, the ivory key holes, brass plate handles and so on, a dating of 1800 would seem quite reasonable, but as already mentioned bureau bookcases had gone out of fashion by 1780 or thereabouts.

The answer to many of these problems lies in the fact that this example was made in the Channel Islands, more specifically in Jersey. The inlay of the cornice is typical of that area, as is the fact that the drawer linings are made of chestnut wood, although the drawer bottoms are made of pine and covered with a thick pale blue paper, a common practice around 1800. The height of the flap is a good 33 inches (838 mm) and, unless one uses a very high chair, writing is quite uncomfortable. It is amazing, therefore, that the feet have not been reduced in size to allow for this. Although there is one minor restoration to the cross-banding on the right-hand door, and one rear foot has been replaced, the amount of damage and wear is slight, indicating that the piece has never been badly treated throughout its life. Although there are ink stains inside the bureau, they are mostly very small and there are none inside the drawers. Some collectors would dismiss such an article as being out of period, but I leave you to draw your own conclusions as to the validity of this criticism.

Having said that bureau bookcases were not made much after 1780, and having stated that this example dates from around 1800, the reader might well ask how such a date could be set. As I have emphasised, dating can only be done from the latest original feature, and that must set the earliest possible date for the piece. Oval plate handles could date from as early as 1795, and the same could be said for the ivory knobs (perhaps five years later) and also the inlaid medallion in the cornice. But perhaps the latest feature is the shaping of the bracket feet, most reminiscent of the splayed bracket feet one associates with a date of about 1800. All these points, combined with the fact that the piece originates from Jersey (it was recently imported), make it difficult to give a date before 1800. Although this piece is provincial, the quality of the dovetails and the choice of timbers indicate that the craftsman was well aware of the best London standards.

A great many bureau bookcases are 'marriages', in other

words the top half does not belong to the bottom, and the reasons for this are quite straightforward. Many years ago bureau bookcases were considered very saleable objects and there was a large public demand for them. Their price therefore rose out of all proportion to their real worth. At the same time bureaux were relatively cheap, so dealers would buy a bureau and make, or adapt, a bookcase top to fit it. They could then sell the 'marriage' for considerably less than the genuine article to the eager home market as well as supplying a flourishing European demand. When examining a two-part piece, careful comparison of the wood used on either half is essential, and a look at the back will also show if mouldings have been altered to accommodate an alien fitment.

It is quite in order for the back of a bureau bookcase to be planked on the lower half and panelled on the top, but it is quite wrong for the top of the bureau to be polished. This can be seen when the bookcase has been removed. Other features, such as mouldings, handles, the matching of escutcheons (provided they have not been replaced) and other minutiae of detail will make it apparent if the pieces started life together. The present example passes all these tests. Occasionally the top half will overhang the back of the bottom half, as the latter had to stand away from the wall because of the skirting board. Some dealers will say this is not the case, and it has even been known for them to reduce the depth of an original top in order to conform with this mistaken notion.

A piece of furniture which was new at the end of the eighteenth century was the sofa table, a rectangular table with a flap at either end. The earlier and more attractive examples had a standard end support to the top of elegant and simple proportions: see the example illustrated in Plate 106. The top of this very good quality piece measures $36\frac{3}{4}$ inches (933 mm) by 24 inches (609 mm), by $27\frac{1}{2}$ inches (694 mm), and when the flaps are raised and supported by their lopers the top measures 59 inches (1448 mm). The present example is in Brazilian or Rio rosewood, cross-banded with East Indian satinwood and outlined with an arrangement of boxwood and ebony. The frieze contains two real and two dummy drawers so that the table looks identical from either side when the drawers are closed. Because the top is supported on its standard ends, either end of the top must be made of a substantial piece of wood which flanks the drawers, and this often has a decorative inlay.

In the present example there is a lozenge of satinwood

106 Rosewood sofa table on standard supports with a high arched stretcher and paw casters, c. 1800.

outlined with boxwood and ebony. Sometimes the central muntin between the drawers gets identical treatment. This example is most unusual in that it has inlay simulating the spine of a book. The standard ends, with their classic outswept legs, are joined in this instance by a high arched stretcher. On later examples this stretcher ran between the lowest point of the standard, while later still, various other complicated arrangements were made to give stability to the design. The legs terminate in brass paw casters. Had the example been slightly earlier it might have had box casters, which are, as the name implies, a simple brass box with the roller wheel beneath. The example illustrated has rounded flaps which are fairly deep, a feature considered desirable, as many flaps are only two-thirds of the depth and present a skimped appearance when they are folded in the vertical position. Sofa tables do exist with square tapered legs at each corner, even with sabre legs, but on early examples the standard end is the classical norm. By the nineteenth century, the standard end had given way to the column or multiple column support in the middle of the table above a platform base.

An essential piece of equipment in any household is a clock, and we have already shown a long-case clock in Plate 7, but a more common method of time-keeping was the bracket clock, an example is illustrated in Plate 96. It is mahogany, and stands 22 inches (559 mm) high. The top is a flattened bell shape and is mounted with brass finials and astragal mould. Below that comes a most delightfully complicated moulding on the main body of the case, which is of carefully chosen mahogany veneers on oak. The front has brass frets backed with red silk, and is flanked by a pair of canted pilasters with brass reeding above an ogee plinth. The base of the clock is brass bound below a cavetto moulding, and the whole sits on ogee brass bracket feet. The sides, as is quite usual, are fitted with shaped apertures with brass grills also backed with red silk.

This clock was, as its name would imply, originally rested on a bracket which hung on the wall. More often than not this bracket is missing, and today most people are happy to let these clocks sit on a piece of furniture.

For the horologically minded, this present example has an eight-day movement with verge escapement, chiming on the quarters. It has a pendulum adjustment dial and a strike/silent dial. The dials are white enamel and signed by 'Walter Mitchelson, London', and the rest of the dial is bright cut and gilded brass; the back plate is similarly decorated and signed inside. It is also fitted with a repeating cord which, when pulled, will strike the previous quarter and hour.

London-made clocks are almost invariably fine quality, and the case-making is, by and large, of a standard superior to that of general cabinet-making. In order to conform with the regulations of the clock-makers' company, it was obligatory for clock-makers to sign their work. As a result of this, one is able to be far more precise about the date than with other furniture. In this instance we know that Walter Mitchelson was working from 1780, and that his address was 3, Helmet Row, London.

The tripod table illustrated in Plate 107 is an example of rustic country-made furniture. The square top is of oak and has four pieces of $\frac{1}{4}$ inch (6 mm) thick oak mould round its edge and mitred at the corners to form a small raised lip. The top is pegged to the frieze which is simply a box opened at one side; the box is held together with hand-made nails and the open side accommodates a drawer with square top edges and thick linings nailed to the front which is fitted with a wooden knob handle. The column is beechwood and of simple tapered form. At the top of the column is a rectangular piece of wood which is chamfered on its end edges and canted so as to show only a small amount at each end. This is pegged to the column. The legs are of ash and slightly cabriole in form; they are of uniform

107 Country-made tripod table, *c.* 1810, fitted with a drawer, made of oak, ash and elm.

thickness and are dovetailed into the base of the column. It is very difficult to assign an accurate date, but an estimate of around 1800 will probably be not far wrong. Certainly the size and overall outline of the base, and the concept of putting a square top of this size on such a piece, is reminiscent of some of the productions of London work of the 1790s. However, the use of pegs for structural security is clearly very archaic, although this has been justified in that this article has remained in fine, sound condition since it was made, there being no signs of the restorer's hand anywhere. The colour and surface are exemplary and there can be no denying that this table has considerable rustic charm. It is also a very useful object.

There are some who may raise their eyebrows at the inclusion of such a piece in this book alongside sophisticated cabinet-made objects. Yet it is just as important to recognise the merits of this table as it is to appreciate, say, the bookcase in Plate 79. They are both unrestored examples of antique English furniture. Whereas one is grand, imposing and of aesthetic and academic interest to the connoisseurs, the other has a delightful warmth and unassuming honesty suitable for the furnishing of a modest house.

The turn of the nineteenth century saw a great revival of interest in the exotic and the East, particularly Egypt, largely as a result of Nelson's victory at the Battle of the Nile.

155

This preoccupation was so intense that it manifested itself in all art forms, including furniture. The table illustrated in Plate 97 is part of a suite of formal state-room furniture of considerable importance dating from around 1815. The top is of Coromandel wood with finely matched figured veneers. The edge has a broad $4\frac{1}{2}$ inch (114 mm) cross-banding within a broad diagonal banding, but otherwise the top is quite plain. The frieze consists of two cross-banded Coromandel bands underlined by a gilded plain moulding, itself supported by three fabulous griffons carved in the round with scrolled tails and each carrying on its head two counterfacing calyxes – these take the weight of the top. The platform base is of concave triangular outline veneered like the top in segments. The plinth is rounded with a knurled decoration in gilt, which is repeated on the scroll feet.

Such a piece is said to have a platform base and is seldom seen before around 1820, although it was known before then and was perhaps first mooted by Thomas Hope when he produced his book of designs in 1807. The present table is large (5 feet 6 inches, 1.7 m in diameter) and is *en suite* with a set of three console tables, one of which can be seen in the background of the picture. Like the console tables mentioned earlier such an object is very typical of the furniture found in grand state apartments in large houses. The average collector could therefore scarcely expect to acquire such a piece, nor indeed would most houses accommodate it. However examples like this help to put more commonplace furniture into its proper perspective and it can be clearly seen how such a table influenced the design of dining tables in succeeding decades. Such tables continued to be made until the second half of the nineteenth century. Construction follows the standard pattern, and the top is supported round its circumference by an apron or frieze up to 3 inches (76 mm) in depth. Usually the top is of good quality timber, oak, or even mahogany, and is, like this example, veneered with an exotic timber or a fine grain mahogany. Interesting and early examples were supported in the same way as this object, but later on a central column was used which enabled the top to tilt on an arrangement of lopers (see Chapter 4). As the tables developed so the central column became larger and more grand, becoming quite grotesque by the middle of the nineteenth century. Coromandel wood was one of a wide variety of highly decorative timbers imported from around 1800 for the next twenty years. It bears a close resemblance to Zebra wood and Calamander. The reason for the patterns on the top was simply that the tree was very narrow and therefore the pattern repeated itself at regular intervals. It is a very dense timber, taking on a glossy polish.

The box-like object illustrated in Plate 108 is a wine cellaret. The top is plain, but beneath it is an interesting and crisp moulding, and the lid has cock beading on its lower edge. It opens to reveal eight divisions designed for bottles, and one long division. The front is panelled with a double cock bead moulding and below are a pair of cupboards similarly decorated. Each panel and the top is of brilliant flame-figured mahogany, and the base moulding is simply reeded. The whole piece stands on turned feet beneath a little bracket. The quality is particularly good, and it is curious that when a piece of antique English furniture has been fitted with carrying handles, the quality is almost always good. The carrying handles in the present example are a completely typical form of a design which remained unchanged for probably fifty years or more. This fact has been known to dealers for a great many years, and occasionally a piece of furniture is 'enhanced' by the addition of handles. However, the present example has original handles and the condition is exceptional throughout; there appears to be no restoration anywhere, and none necessary. The surface is well polished and has obviously been the subject of lavish attention for a very considerable period of time.

Red wine, brought up from the cellar in a bottle carrier, would be stored in such a cellaret in the dining-room, standing at room temperature for several days. The cupboard beneath was probably intended for the numerous other accessories available at the time this piece was made, for example a punch bowl, ladle, wine taster, bottle labels and so on. A bottle cradle and coasters could also have been kept inside, though these may well have been left on the sideboard with their attendant decanters in them. But most likely the cupboard contained a chamber pot. Such an article was obligatory in any well-equipped dining room, where the gentlemen would have been confined for some time after the ladies left at the end of a meal.

Many people imagine that all antiques must be beautiful, but this piece of furniture surely proves them wrong. In contrast to the concertina card table illustrated in Plate 84, this has all the attributes a collector could wish for – originality of design, superb craftsmanship, exemplary condition – and it is functional. Nonetheless, the reader may feel that this piece is very 'boxy' in appearance and of no particularly aesthetic line.

It should be noted in passing that had the interior of this article been lined with lead, it would have been a wine cooler.

The distinction between a cellaret and cooler is that the latter is designed to contain white wine at a cold temperature. Ice was packed into the lead-lined divisions and, when it melted, the water was let out through a tap fitted below.

It has been my intention, in selecting examples of antique English furniture, to show a wide range of styles, qualities and condition. The set of chairs illustrated in Plate 109 represents the humblest form of English furniture which can be classed as genuine antique. Doubtless I will be shown numerous even more rustic examples of antique furniture, but this set of chairs will serve to make a point. The entire set is made of ash, in itself a cheap substitute for oak, but the style clearly indicates that mahogany was the fashionable ideal. Fruitwoods, particularly cherry, have a reddish hue more closely approximating to mahogany and had this been used the colour would have enhanced this design.

The backs are slightly curved, and in both directions, which is a pleasing feature. The stiles are moulded and the one concession to decoration on the top rail is a roll-over effect created by a chip being taken from the rear edge. The double bar middle rail enclosing three balls is reminiscent of Suffolk-made chairs, often called Mendelsham chairs. The seat is narrow, measuring only $17\frac{1}{2}$ inches (440 mm) wide and $13\frac{1}{4}$ inches (340 mm) deep – compare this with the Chippendale chairs in Plate 3, which are $22\frac{1}{2}$ inches (572 mm) by $17\frac{1}{2}$ inches (445 mm). The wooden seat is fixed to its rails with three nails on each side, and the marks are hidden with putty. The insides of the seat rails clearly betray the marks of the pit-saw, and the undersides are darker where hands have left dirty marks. The front legs are turned and all the legs are joined by stretchers. Two of the chairs slope very considerably and many of the seats are asymmetrical. At first, one might think this was due to the use of unseasoned timber, but in fact it is faulty chair-making. Fortunately there are six chairs rather than a smaller number, but one, while very similar, is not an exact match with the others.

Country-made furniture is usually very difficult to date accurately, but from the design of these chairs, and in particular the overhanging top rail which made its appearance at about the turn of the nineteenth century, it would be impossible to date these before about 1810. However, it is far more likely that they were made fifteen or even thirty years later than this. The chairs retain their original colour and patination, and are typical of the large quantity of genuine, if unimportant, rustic chairs available in the antique market today. While having no grandiose pretentions, they are ideal cottage furniture, and also have the considerable merit of being inexpensive.

109 Matched set of six ash dining chairs, country crafted, and of meagre proportions dating from about 1820-30.

Chapter 7

The market place

There are many people who can give advice on antique furniture and the reader should approach different authorities according to the kind of information required. The commercial aspect is catered for primarily by dealers and auctioneers, while the academic side is looked after by museum staff, lecturers and writers. Then there are other interested people who fall into neither of these categories, who furnish their homes with old English furniture – the collectors and those who have lived with good furniture all their lives and are knowledgeable about what they have. A word of explanation of each of these groups may perhaps be helpful.

The term 'antique dealer' is grossly over-used. A large number of shops which claim to sell antiques have perhaps only two or three items over 100 years old in their stock, the remainder being made up of more recent and second-hand items of varying quality and aesthetic merit. At the other end of the scale are dealers of considerable knowledge and integrity, keeping their stocks of specialised and fine quality items at expensive addresses in London, New York, Paris, or wherever. Very often the dealer discovers things unknown to the academic, and the reverse is also most certainly true. A glass dealer recently pointed out to me that green decanters are rare but green glasses are common, while blue decanters are common and blue glasses are rare. An academic is unlikely to provide such information, but a person who regularly buys and sells will soon make this kind of observation.

In Great Britain there are two organisations of dealers. First, there is the British Antique Dealers' Association (BADA) with a membership numbering approximately 500, of whom more than half are in London. These dealers tend to be specialists in their chosen spheres. Second, there is the more recently formed London and Provincial Antique Dealers' Association (LAPADA). Both these organisations will supply information concerning their membership on request, and among their number are most British dealers of repute.

When owners wish to sell something they may well choose to send it to auction rather than sell it direct to a dealer. The auctioneer merely acts as an agent for the vendors and will hold sales at more or less regular intervals for this purpose. The larger auction houses have regular sales at frequent intervals and may also have specialist sales in particular subjects. Firms with a large turnover have specialist sales as often as once a week. The London market is dominated by two firms, but the remainder are now perhaps catching a larger percentage of the market owing to the fact that these two houses charge a commission to the purchaser as well as to the vendor.

As with the leading dealers, the leading auctioneers have formed themselves into an association called the Society of Fine Art Auctioneers (SOFAA). Most auctioneers charge commission on a sliding scale varying between 10 and 20 per cent to the vendor. Where, however, the commission is charged to the purchaser as well, the vendor's commission is usually a flat 10 per cent. There are some areas in the provinces where auctioneers charge a commission to the purchaser; these include parts of Cornwall, South Devon and Lincolnshire.

Museum staff will often be most helpful in establishing the nature and date of an object, but they are bound to avoid any commercial consideration. The bigger museums have the finest reference libraries available on matters concerning furniture, silver and porcelain, and many books have been written by those who look after our national collections. For example, a considerable amount of research has been done recently by the staff of the Victoria and Albert Museum on the arrangement of furniture – the history and evolution of where furniture was placed in a room. Much work has also been done concerning the correct methods of upholstery, the way a chair is stuffed and how a bed is hung. Few dealers have this kind of information, for the number of eighteenth-century chairs to appear on the market with their original upholstery is negligible. Most such examples are either still in the houses for which they were originally constructed or else in museums. Such objects present problems commercially, since chairs covered in material which is 200 years old cannot be used for their original purpose, namely for sitting on. Nevertheless they do have an enormous value to the academic, and this example highlights the disparity of interest between dealers and museum staff.

Anyone who decided to furnish his house with, say, 'French Hepplewhite' furniture and was able to devote a considerable proportion of his energies to studying this type of furniture would soon know a vast amount about a very limited subject. It is therefore quite feasible that a person who is in no way professionally concerned with the antiques market may be an acknowledged expert in a particular field. A great many collectors have formed themselves into clubs, which operate throughout the country; and the members of these clubs meet at regular intervals to discuss and to hear talks by their colleagues and by visiting speakers. Some of these people are very knowledgeable indeed.

When buying or selling furniture, one has three options. First, one may sell privately, for example to a friend or acquaintance. If this course of action is preferred then it is a good idea to have the article valued first by an independent expert. Second, one may sell at auction. This will generally take a few weeks, or months if it is rare and of special interest and is to be included in a specialist sale, but the price achieved is the highest bid less the commission. Third, one may sell to a dealer, in which case one will normally be paid immediately, unless one sells on a commission basis. Most dealers of good repute are sufficiently jealous of their reputation not to pay too little, but the seller may well feel that more could have been achieved. On the other hand, it must be remembered that by far the largest proportion of goods sold at auction are purchased by dealers and it is unusual to buy something at auction at the top bid one is prepared to pay.

The same arguments apply when buying. Most dealers will maintain a stock of furniture which they bought at auction at prices below those which they were prepared to pay. Purchasing from a reputable dealer is probably the best way of safeguarding oneself against doing the wrong thing, but of course one will be paying a share of the profit and overheads. If the dealer is a member of BADA there is a built-in arbitration system in the very unlikely event of there being any dispute about the object. Buying from a less élite establishment may well be cheaper, but the safeguards are not there. Buying at auctions also has its drawbacks. If one is fully cognisant of the market value of the things one is interested in and knows precisely what one is about, then it may well be less expensive than buying from a dealer. One or two points, however, do emerge. Some dealers make only marginal profits and bidding one more bid than a dealer may not necessarily be cheaper than letting the dealer buy the article first and then sell it to you.

People often wonder how it is that dealers can manage to buy from each other, and the trade is often accused of escalating prices in a heady spiral. Perhaps this criticism has some validity but in practice it should be viewed in another way. There is a kind of pyramidal structure in dealing. At the base of the pyramid are thousands of bric-à-brac shops; above that, shops where the occasional antique is to be found; further up, and correspondingly fewer in number, are dealers who maintain stocks of presentable antiques; while at the apex are the exclusive specialists.

Any object placed on the market will find its own level within this pyramidal structure. Sometimes, of course, the first purchaser sells retail, but if, shall we say, a fine set of twelve Chippendale chairs were to be bought by a bric-à-brac merchant, it is unlikely that intending buyers would be looking for them in such an establishment. More likely, they would peruse the shop windows of the West End. Meanwhile, the West End dealer will not waste time searching countless thousands of bric-à-brac shops, but will call upon a very select number of shops which occasionally have more valuable or specialist objects.

The bric-à-brac merchant will be visited by dealers who buy antiques in a general way and they in turn will be visited by dealers who specialise in furniture. The chairs will therefore quickly pass through these three hands. The furniture dealer may then sell them to a provincial dealer who specialises in antique furniture and it is probably this person upon whom the West End dealer will call. Thus the chairs will find their level within the market, and it is for this very reason that it is possible to buy bargains from a dealer.

To conclude: if one knows exactly what one is about when selling, then one is best advised to go to a dealer and ask for a particular price. If one is uncertain then it may be better to risk perhaps 15 per cent commission and sell at an auction house. When buying, unless one is fully aware of values, it would be much safer to use a dealer.

It must be remembered that auctioneers receive their commission in most instances from the vendor and their allegiance must lie firmly in that quarter. Most auctioneers will proffer opinions as to how much an object is likely to make, but valuation is a most inexact science and that, together with the auctioneer's allegiance, should be taken into careful consideration, particularly with an expensive object.

Glossary

Acanthus Stylised leaf decoration, derived from classical ornament.

Anthemion Stylised honeysuckle motif, commonly used in Neo-classical designs.

Apron A downward extension below what would normally be the bottom edge (e.g. the seat of a chair or the frame of a cabinet).

Arcading A line of ornamental arches, found particularly on oak furniture.

Aumbry Medieval or Gothic cupboard, originally for storing alms, but often used for storing food.

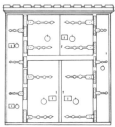

Bail A curved, hanging pull for drawers, etc., usually with a back plate.

Baluster A short pillar, often in the shape of a vase.

Banding A flat, ornamental or veneered border around a door, panel, drawer or table. In cross-banding, the grain runs at right angles to the edge; feather banding and herring-bone bandings are arranged in a continuing chevron pattern, and are normally confined to walnut furniture.

Barley twist Turning in a spiral to give the effect of a twisted column.

Beadwork A decoration on material employing brightly coloured glass beads, which unlike needlework is resistant to fading.

Bevel A slope cut at the edge of a flat surface, most commonly the angled edge of plate glass and mirrors.

Bird-cage A device used in eighteenth-century tripod tables, resembling a cage with vertical bars, which allows the table to revolve as well as tip (page 39).

Bonheur-du-jour A small, writing table of French derivation, with a superstructure containing drawers and cupboards.

Box toilet mirror A mirror mounted on a box-like frame containing small drawers.

Bracket foot A shaped foot used in carcase furniture, projecting slightly from the corner.

Bonheur-du-jour

Canterbury

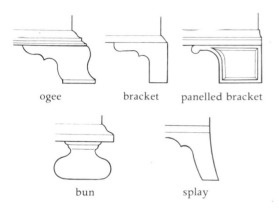

ogee   bracket   panelled bracket

bun   splay

Types of feet

Carlton House desk

Bun foot A flattened ball foot, used on furniture from the mid-seventeenth century.

Bureau A desk with a lid sloping at an angle of about 45° that folds out as a writing table, with drawers beneath.

Cabochon Domed decoration, in particular a raised oval surrounded by a rim.

Cabriole leg A leg curving outwards at the top or knee and tapering in an elongated 'S' towards the foot.

Camel-back A chair of which the top rail is shaped like a Cupid's bow; exaggerated serpentine.

Canted Obliquely faced.

Canterbury A stand with slated partitions, usually with a drawer, for holding sheet music.

Carcase furniture A general term for furniture used for storage, as distinct from chairs or tables.

Carlton House desk A late eighteenth-century writing table in mahogany or satinwood of the type commissioned for the Prince of Wales' residence, with a D-shaped superstructure of small drawers and pigeonholes.

Cartouche A tablet, normally in the form of a curling scroll or shield, to accommodate inscriptions or armorial devices.

Caster A small, swivelling wheel attached to the leg of a piece of furniture.

Channel moulding Term applied to grooved decoration of uniform cross section in early oak furniture. Usually on the inside edge of a panel frame.

Claw-and-ball A carved, ornamental foot in vogue during the eighteenth century.

Cleat A strip of wood fixed to the end of a flat surface to provide additional strength.

Corbel A supporting projection of bracket form

Countersink To cut a bevelled hole to conceal a screw head.

165

Cup-and-cover A bulbous, turned decoration, often elaborately carved and found on the legs of Elizabethan furniture. The top half is frequently gadrooned.

Davenport A small writing desk often with a moving shallow-sloped top.

Dentils A decorative row of small squares.

Distressing A euphemism for superficial damage.

Dovetail A wood joint consisting of a series of interlocking wedge-shaped projections.

Drum table A circular table with drawers, sometimes revolving.

Ear A shaped block of wood applied on either side at the top of a cabriole leg.

Egg-and-dart (egg-and-tongue) A moulding in the form of alternating ovals and wedges.

En suite Matching; part of a series.

Escritoire A cabinet on a chest of drawers or stand, with a drop front writing surface.

Fall front (drop front) The writing surface of a desk or cabinet, which has to be lowered for use.

Figure A general term for the pattern in wood.

Fillet A narrow strip of wood.

Finial A vase, spike or other ornament projecting upwards.

Fluting Ornamentation of close-set, semi-circular, concave grooves.

Fly-leg A leg without stretchers, swivelling to support a table top.

Frieze The horizontal member supporting a cornice, table or bench top, etc.

Fluting

Froe See Riving iron.

Gadrooning A decorative moulding of consecutive convex, or alternating concave and convex curves.

Gallery In furniture, a decorative low railing, usually openwork.

Garya husk (or bell flower) A stylised flower form, like a wheat husk or bluebell, found as carved or inlaid decoration in Neo-classical and 'French Hepplewhite' furniture.

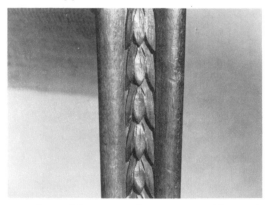

Gate-leg table A circular or oval table, with flaps supported by 'gates' which swing out from the central section.

Gesso A composition material like plaster, usually painted or gilded.

Guilloche Decorative pattern of intertwined circles, usually Neo-classical (opposite top).

Hutch See Aumbry.

Key pattern A geometrical pattern of straight lines and right angles, reminiscent of a maze.

Linenfold A carved ornamentation imitating folded cloth, popular up to about 1570.

Lining The sides and back of a drawer.

Lopers Wooden runners that support a fall front or table top.

Lowboy A table with a symmetrical arrangement of drawers round a knee-hole.

Lozenge A diamond pattern with a horizontal long axis.

Lunette A carved fan-shaped motif.

Marquetry An ornamental pattern on surfaces of furniture made by fitting together pieces of different coloured woods, shell, ivory, metal, etc., into a single sheet which is applied to the surface.

Medallion An oval, circular or square device.

Medullary rays In timber, lines that radiate outwards from the centre crossing the rings. Sometimes visible in oak.

Mitre A corner joint, in which the line of the join appears to besect the angle.

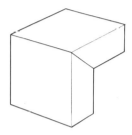

Mortise and tenon A joint in which a rectangular cavity (mortise) in one section receives the projecting tongue (tenon) of the other.

Moulding A shaped strip of uniform cross-section, sometimes carved, applied as decoration or to conceal joints.

Muntin A vertical wooden member between two panels.

Ogee An elongated 'S' shape, as found in bracket feet, arches and mouldings.

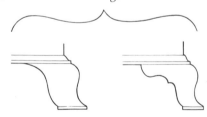

Ormolu Strictly, gilt bronze, but often applied to lacquered or gilt brass.

Pad foot A rounded foot similar to the club foot, the two terms being often interchangeable.

Panel A shaped or rectangular member framed by stiles, rails and often muntins.

Papier-mâché A material consisting of mashed paper combined with a binding agent and various other substances, which hardens when dry.

Patera A Neo-classical design, oval or round, frequently resembling a flower or rosette.

Pediment An architectural or scrolled member on the top of carcase furniture.

Pendant Any form of suspended ornament.

Pie-crust A raised shaped edging resembling a pie-crust.

Pilaster An applied decoration in the form of a flat-sided column.

Plate handle A handle with a protective backing.

Plywood A composition usually of three veneers glued together, the grain of each running at right angles to the others to prevent warping and give extra strength. Used mainly for galleries or tray rims.

Pole screen A firescreen mounted on a pole, usually with a tripod or platform base.

Rail A horizontal member in cabinet-making.

Rebate A groove (also called a rabbet).

Reeding Decoration of consecutive convex curves often seen on legs and as an edging.

Re-entrant corner A rounded corner incorporating a cusp.

Riving iron (Froe) A medieval tool used for splitting wood into planks.

Rococo A European art style developed from the Baroque, characterised by a profusion of scrolls, shells, foliage, icicles and rockwork.

Roundel Any circular ornament.

Rule joint A stopped and quarter-moulded joint, which allows a table leaf to fold without leaving a gap.

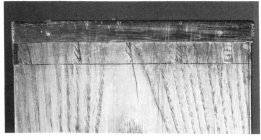

Scribing line Mark inscribed by a cabinet-maker in preparation for cutting joints.

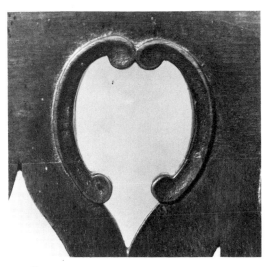

Scrolling

Scroll Curving or spiral decoration.

Secretaire Writing furniture with a drawer the front of which lets down to provide a flat surface.

Shield-back Chair design made fashionable by Hepplewhite in which the rail and stile form the shape of a shield.

Shoe-piece A bar at the base of a chair back into which the central splat was slotted.

Shoulder See Ear.

Slope front See Fall-front.

Splat A vertical member between the seat and top rail of a chair.

Split Baluster A form of decoration used in the seventeenth century where turning is cut in half along its length and applied to a surface.

Stile A vertical member forming the side of a frame.

Strap work Stylised representation of geometrically arranged leather straps.

Straw work A method of decoration employing small slivers of straw, often coloured.

Strap work

Stretcher A member linking and supporting legs of furniture.

Striation Striped imperfection.

Stringing A narrow inlaid strip of light or dark contrasting timber, or of brass.

Stumpwork A seventeenth-century form of embroidery, partly in relief.

Swan-neck An ogee curve applied to handles and pediments.

Tallboy (Chest on chest) A tall chest of drawers in two sections, one above the other.

Teapoy A small piece of furniture with a hinged lid, incorporating tea-caddies, mixing bowls and other accessories.

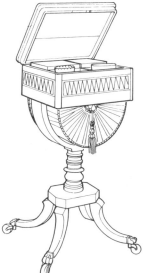

Terminal The end of a chair arm, on which the hand rests.

Tracheid Fibres in timber which produce the grain.

Turning A form of decoration achieved by the use of a lathe.

Veneer A thin sheet of wood, normally of decorative figure, applied to a timber base.

Volute A spiral scroll.

Whatnot A stand of square or rectangular shelves, sometimes incorporating one or two drawers.

Woods

Amboyna A rich, honey-coloured timber used from about 1780. It always has a very pronounced burr figure.

Beech When freshly cut, a pale cream, close-grained wood showing very definite, but very small, medullary rays. Most commonly used for seat rails and in country furniture. On objects older than 200 years, it becomes a dull indistinctive brown. Its ability to take nails and have them removed makes it very suitable for upholstery and this accounts for the many objects for which it is used that appear in this book.

Burrs Undoubtedly the hardest woods to identify are those displaying a burr figure. Most experts have considerable difficulty distinguishing between burr walnut, elm, ash, yew, amboyna and pollard oak. The practised eye will look for a small area of wood where the burr is absent and one will hope to identify the grain at that point to determine what the rest is.

Calamander, Coromandel and Zebra wood These three woods were used from around 1790 as veneers and are all very stripy black to ginger yellow. They are very hard dense grained timbers taking on a brilliant polish. The three woods are frequently confused and for our purposes the easiest distinction is the proportion of light and dark. Zebra wood is predominantly light with dark streaks, coromandel has an almost even distribution of both, while calamander has light streaks on a black ground.

Fruitwoods (Apple, Cherry and Pear) These are pale brown, medium lightweight close grained woods, and are used in country-made furniture. Pale pear was used as a banding and as a ground for lacquer work in the late seventeenth century. The redder cherry is occasionally used decoratively.

Harewood Green or green/brown stained sycamore (see separate entry).

Holly Pale straw-coloured dense hard wood used as a decorative inlay in the sixteenth and seventeenth centuries and as a substitute for boxwood in the eighteenth. Also used as the ground for inlaid shells, medallions, paterae, etc.

Kingwood In the seventeenth century called Princes Wood, and used as an oyster veneer usually cut on the slant so that the oyster was oval. From 1770 frequently used as cross-banding. Very hard close-grained, brown tending slightly to mauve.

Laburnum Hard, dense wood with sapwood of almost equal density to the heart. The heart is deep chocolate brown, the sap a pale yellow. Used decoratively, often in chevron veneers to emphasise the colour contrast.

Lignum vitae An exceptionally dense hard dark nut-brown wood, frequently used for lathe turning of ornaments and utensils called Treen. Seldom used in cabinet-making.

Padouk (spelt Padauk in America) A very hard and heavy timber. When freshly cut it has a distinct violet hue, but it mellows to a mid nut brown and in sunlight will fade to a rich honey. Has very little figure and a wild grain and is most frequently found on furniture from around 1720-70. Usually employed in the solid.

Purpleheart When freshly cut a brilliant purple colour, but mellowing to chocolate brown, usually displaying slight whitish streaks in the grain. Used as a banding (seldom cross-banding) mainly from around 1770-1800.

Sycamore A soft pale yellow/straw timber often displaying fiddleback figure, used as a decorative inlay when it can closely resemble satinwood in appearance. Stained with iron oxide to a greeny brown, it is called Harewood and used principally on fine quality furniture 1770-1800.

Tulipwood When freshly cut tulipwood is a pale straw colour with magenta streaks. These mellow, leaving the wood a striated deep straw colour used extensively in French furniture as a ground veneer and in England as a cross-banding. Yellower and paler than Kingwood, these two timbers constitute the vast proportion of cross-bandings in furniture between 1770 and 1800.

Yew A dense, closely grained softwood usually of contorted grain and figure with tones ranging from ginger through brown to a slight purple tint. Very seldom used as a decorative veneer, but commonly employed for the decorative members of Windsor chairs. Burr yew used as a decorative inlay from the latter half of the eighteenth century.

(The dates are approximate)

	1550	1560	1570	1580	1590	1600	1610	1620	1630	1640	1650	1660	1670

Kings and Queens

———————— Elizabeth I ———————— James I ———— Charles I ———— Common-wealth (Cromwell) ——— Charles II

– – – – — Tudor ———————— Stuart – – – –

Furniture Names

Design Influences

Renaissance

Introduction of

Coffer   Buffet   Gate-leg Table   Chest of Drawers
Bed   Dining Chairs   Longcase clock
Cupboard   Bookcase
Mirrors

Timbers

——— Oak ———————————————————— – – – –

Walnut – – – – – – – – – – – ——— Solid

Other Materials

Lacquer ———

Gilding

Decoration Details

Linenfold   Romayne Head   'Nonesuch' Inlay   Lunettes ⎤
                                   Arcading   Lozenges ⎦

	1550	1560	1570	1580	1590	1600	1610	1620	1630	1640	1650	1660	1670

in the history of furniture

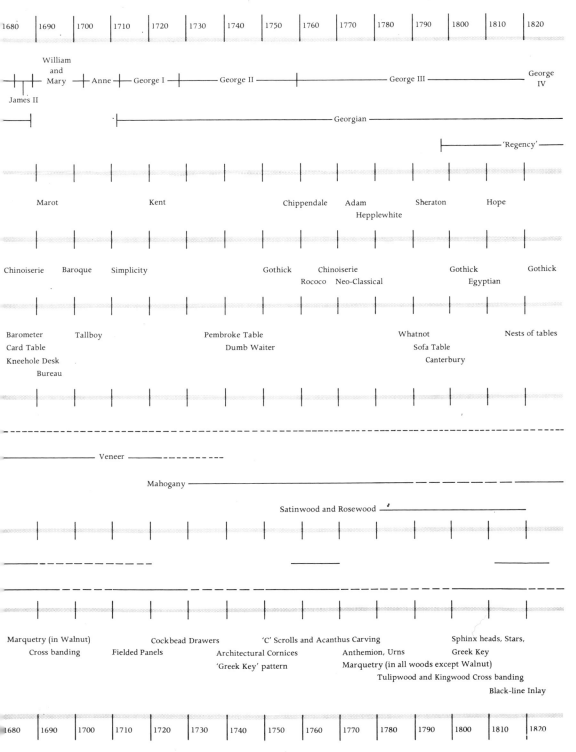

1680 | 1690 | 1700 | 1710 | 1720 | 1730 | 1740 | 1750 | 1760 | 1770 | 1780 | 1790 | 1800 | 1810 | 1820

William and Mary

James II

Anne — George I — George II — George III — George IV

Georgian

'Regency'

Marot   Kent   Chippendale   Adam   Sheraton   Hope
Hepplewhite

Chinoiserie   Baroque   Simplicity   Gothick   Chinoiserie   Gothick   Gothick
Rococo   Neo-Classical   Egyptian

Barometer   Tallboy   Pembroke Table   Whatnot   Nests of tables
Card Table   Dumb Waiter   Sofa Table
Kneehole Desk   Canterbury
Bureau

Veneer

Mahogany

Satinwood and Rosewood

Marquetry (in Walnut)   Cockbead Drawers   'C' Scrolls and Acanthus Carving   Sphinx heads, Stars,
Cross banding   Fielded Panels   Architectural Cornices   Anthemion, Urns   Greek Key
'Greek Key' pattern   Marquetry (in all woods except Walnut)
Tulipwood and Kingwood Cross banding
Black-line Inlay

1680 | 1690 | 1700 | 1710 | 1720 | 1730 | 1740 | 1750 | 1760 | 1770 | 1780 | 1790 | 1800 | 1810 | 1820

Bibliography

This is a short selection of the books I have found most useful in the course of both my work and in writing this book. They fall into several categories, as follows.

Early standard reference works containing numerous photographs and mainly published between 1880 and 1925. An enormous amount has been learnt about English furniture since these books were written and, although they make very interesting reading and illustrate some pieces which have long since been lost, they must be read in the context of the limited knowledge available at the time. They are now out of print and are not therefore generally available but may possibly be found in second-hand book shops and established libraries:

English Furniture of the Eighteenth Century H. Cescinsky (3 vols.)

English Decoration and Furniture of the Early Renaissance M. Jourdan

Early English Furniture and Woodwork H. Cescinsky and E. Gribble

History of English Furniture: 1. *The Age of Oak* 2. *The Age of Walnut* 3. *The Age of Mahogany* 4. *The Age of Satinwood* P. Macquoid

The Dictionary of English Furniture P. Macquoid and R. Edwards

More modern general books about English furniture.

The Dictionary of English Furniture, 2nd edition. P. Macquoid and R. Edwards, Country Life 1954

The Shorter Dictionary of English Furniture R. Edwards, Hamlyn 1964

English Furniture Maurice Tomlin, Faber 1972

English Furniture Styles Ralph Fastnedge, Penguin 1969

Most books dealing with a particular period of English cabinet-making can be relied upon to give helpful information. These include:

Furniture in England Samuel W. Wolsey and R. W. P. Luff, Arthur Barker 1968

Chippendale Furniture Anthony Coleridge, Faber 1968

Regency Furniture Clifford Musgrave, Faber 1971

Sheraton Furniture Ralph Fastnedge, Faber 1962

Nineteenth Century English Furniture Elizabeth Aslin, Faber 1962

Victorian Furniture R. W. Symonds and B. B. Whineray, Country Life 1962

Facsimile copies of eighteenth-century master works:

The Gentleman and Cabinet Maker's Director Thomas Chippendale, Dover Publications

The Cabinet Maker's and Upholsterer's Guide George Hepplewhite, Dover Publications 1970

The Cabinet Maker's and Upholsterer's Drawing Book Thomas Sheraton, Dover Publications 1971

Other related works:

Directory of Historic Cabinet Woods F. L. Hinckley, Crown 1960

English Barometers and Their Makers Nicholas Goodson, Antique Collectors' Club 1977

Old Clocks and Watches and their makers F. J. Britten, Eyre Methuen 1973

English Looking glasses Geoffrey Wills, Country Life 1965

Treen and Other Wooden Bygones Edward Pinto, G. Bell 1969

Directory of Tools used in the Woodworking and Allied Trades R. A. Salaman, Allen and Unwin 1975

English Decoration in the Eighteenth Century John Fowler and John Cornforth, Barrie and Jenkins 1974

Museum guides and the journals of appropriate learned societies. For example, The Victoria & Albert Museum guides, i.e. English Chairs, English Desks and Bureaux, etc. The journals of the Furniture History Society for the more advanced student.

Index

Acknowledgements

The photographs in this book were taken by Robert
Du Pontet for the Hamlyn Group with the exception of those
on the pages listed below:

A. C. Cooper, London 70; Hamlyn Group Picture Library
10, 24, 132 right, 165 centre right; Hotspur, London 18, 19,
20, 21, 25, 28; Victoria and Albert Museum,
London 11, 17 top, 23.
Line drawings by The Hayward Art Group.